G000117594

ALWAYS CRASHING

ISSUE FOUR

CHICAGO, ILLINOIS • PITTSBURGH, PENNSYLVANIA

Copyright 2021 Always Crashing. All rights to the works published herein remain with the individual authors.

ISBN: 978-0-578-88558-2

Always Crashing is a magazine of fiction, poetry, and nameless things around and in-between. We publish one print issue per year and feature online content year-round. We are headquartered in Chicago, Illinois, and Pittsburgh, Pennsylvania.

Editors: Jessica Berger & James Tadd Adcox

Managing Editor: Helenmary Sheridan

The editors wish to thank Matthew Kosinski, Gesina Phillips, Emily Kiernan, and Elayne Sheridan for their generous support.

Always Crashing is reader supported: we do not charge submission fees from writers, and we receive no institutional support. If you'd like to find out more about supporting *Always Crashing*, please visit our Patreon page: www.patreon.com/alwayscrashingmag

For submission guidelines, ordering information, and access to our electronic edition featuring new work every two weeks, please visit www.alwayscrashing.com

SIDE A

SIDE B

/ / /

/ side a

DANGEROUS

/ Catherine Gammon

1

It can be dangerous to know a thing, a solitary place. To hold one's breath as a way of shouting. The irresistible tendency to crystalize myth, to manufacture harmony and offer it to others, cunningly rat-proofed, stylish and reasonable, to conceal disorder, too much trouble to stand, to rouse a will, a voice, a terminological gathering, various and nocturnal, so much simpler to collapse, hostile and righteous with caring, sweeping, mopping. Things got ugly quickly, the poet[1] said, and went on from there to write a brilliant and famous poem. Things got ugly quickly and every day now they get ugly, with now and then a reprieve.

2

The willingness to erase multitudes, the futility of the commons, inextricable, inexhaustible, diminish the capacity for fate, for prophecy and warning—disaster isolate. Moldering books in bookish wastes, cordoned off, preserved, hoard a plague of fragile misjudgments, in rigorous argument and mourning pages deriding challengers and facile converts, their inadequacy, their contours, their stumbles and missteps. Barriers deprived cede ground. Upheavals spur and lag, their prickly switchbacks fracturing, fragmenting in dead ends. Where do we go from here? she asks, and gets no answer, but stands in rain and wind to listen just the same.

3

No one can do it for us, momentary insight, walk on water. Many Americans may not know their own collaborationist cunning, ambiguity and interpretation, the cult of nothing missing, nothing hidden. What is your reference system? Sequential, logical, overpowered. Paris, midnight. Where do you find yourself? Inexorable

---

1   See Terrance Hayes's "American Sonnet for the New Year," *The New Yorker*, January 7, 2019.

dimensions, clever amplitudes, righteous impartialities. A world without high-heeled shoes and ruby lip gloss, right in the heart of the ancient city. The community demanded a meeting so a meeting was held. The cat is healthy. He takes comfort in your laundry basket.

4

Why make things, when the earth gives magnolias, death cap mushrooms, shield volcanoes, acidified oceans, caribou? Why be a litter wizard when on every street corner you find a spent syringe? Voice from a nightmare, an ecstatic cascade: People should be scared, it says, obsessive in their breathtaking specificity, delighted, disarmed. Meltwater wreaking havoc, disappearing ice, sheets become a lens. Why make things? Do not force my hand, says the man, steely, handsome, innocent. Or not. Ask a few necessary questions. Not a subscriber? Overlooked? Unclassifiable? Learn the skills and tools you need. Start seedlings.

5

My mother sitting on the edge of her bed, as if waiting for a train, asked what she's waiting for, answers, "Death." When I was a child I walked in cold tide pools poking a tiny finger into the mouths of red anemones. I stumble on the word—*anemone*, not *anenome*. An enemy, a fact, the outcome of the notorious election. *The Lord is my shepherd, I shall not want.* A cloud of sweetness surrounds the first cut daffodils. She sits on the edge of her bed. *The Lord is my shepherd*— Hot red chilis, sesame oil, and miso permeate and ferment cubed tofu until it's soft and creamy. *I shall not want.* "For death," she says. Anenome, anemone. *The Lord is my*— as into the chapel silence at the county jail through the PA system a voice screeches violently its mundane request. *I shall not*—

INSIDE THE CAVE

/ Jennifer Lynn Christie

In the hills of this unnamed paradise (anonymous to protect our identities), every family's child lived off an undead inheritance, until the walls around her caved in.

This was me.

School wasn't going well. I was too smart. You could put in me a quantum mechanics class, but I'd already dreamt up all the answers in my sleep as a teen. In dreams, everything between all the realms and force fields and dimensions slicked out to a precise point on my forehead, God's drishti, the micro to God's macro, the place God looked to keep from falling over. So, science and art, and all that, it wasn't working out for me, because I already knew what the professors were going to say before they said it. Everyone around me was learning, and I was bored. I was deemed a full-blown distraction by teachers and pupils alike. I would start mouthing the very words that were coming out of the lecturer's mouth, and then I'd be saying it out loud, too, in tandem:

"...in the microworld, there are neither waves, nor particles, or so far as we know—there is only phenomena. If you think of phenomena in relation to the measurement of their contexts, we can predict wavelike distributions. But this is in appearance only. Certain apparatuses will bring wavelike affects, but others will appear particlelike. Nothing is intrinsic in the microworld, from mechanics to chromodynamics. Nothing is indistinguishable."

That kind of thing.

They kicked me out. No one at home understood what it was all about.

"Why don't you just be quiet when the guy's talking?" asked my mother.

"Well, I just feel all this rage," I said. "I feel like if he doesn't shut up, something he doesn't even know about might smite him down."

"You be careful who you say this stuff to," my mother said, "you're going to scare someone. You're scarin' me!" She was always at the cutting board, cutting all these little vegetables, making snack packs for meetings.

Dad was out back, grilling up some meat. One year for Father's Day I gave him a card that said, "You're the rarest of them all," and anyone in the room could have seen that his whole life had happened so that he could live to see that day.

"You've been in school too long," he shouted from the back porch to where we were in the kitchen. "Graduate already!"

He was right. I had been in college for seven years, hopping around, infuriated, thinking I'd stumble upon the one thing I knew nothing about. But I knew everything.

I dropped out of all my classes and wrote a long thesis on the nature of the cosmos as seen though the lens of a microscope and addressed the finished product to the dean of the university. He read it, liked it well enough, and agreed to give me an honorary degree, as long as I managed to stay out of any graduating ceremonies, and never returned to campus. They sent my degree in the mail, a laminated piece of plastic that looked about the size of a library card. I didn't think it would be good for anything, but, for the first time in a long time, I was wrong. My little degree got me into some of the hottest clubs and VIP scenarios (e.g. movie premieres/screenings, backstage passes to concerts, important meetings with business moguls). I didn't think I would indulge in any of these distractions, but finally, I dolled up, and went out on the town.

Looking back, I know this is when my little incubator started to lose some of its steam.

Though it didn't seem that way at the time. As I sat alone at the premiere to a movie called *Monks Alive!* the man sitting in front of me turned around and said, "Olivia Park."

I removed my sunglasses and said, "Do I know you?" and he said, "Mark Drabble," and I knew him immediately as the journalism student I dated for a second my first sophomore year of college (not to be confused with my second and third sophomore years, each one distinct and shattering). He was in a suit and tie and looked like a young Bob Dylan.

"Mark Drabble," I said, so that he knew I recognized him.

"I drabble and I dabble," he said, repeating his insane little article-writer's catch phrase/failed flirter's pick-up line that he had used as an undergraduate. He was tacky.

I leaned forward in my seat and said, "Don't say that to me," and then, "So, looks like you graduated, too."

"I graduated three years ago, Olivia. Right on time."

"Well, don't rub it in. Did you follow your dreams?"

Mark shrugged. "I guess. I wanted to be a contributor to the *Hills Times* but instead found myself at the *Star Reporter*. Not investigative journalism, but not the tabloids either."

I snickered. "Barely." I crossed my legs and leaned back in my seat. I don't know why it felt so good to be mean to the man. Probably because he was condescending, like all of my male college colleagues, especially the ones who got hired right away. The ones who had jobs before they even got their diplomas. Then I leaned back forward and said into his ear, "Just so you know, I don't know anything about you, and I don't want to."

He reached over the back of his art house theater chair and put his hand on my bare leg. "Hey," he said, "what are you doing later?" I put my hand on his shoulder and told him the truth: "Sleeping for sixteen hours on my scream pillow." My scream pillow was the pillow I was allowed to scream into during fits of existential angst while stewing in my girlhood bedroom, so as not to awaken my parents.

"Listen," he continued, as if I were flirting back, "would you like to get together after this? Maybe not tonight, but, maybe tomorrow?"

"No," I said. After a good sleep 'n scream, I was going to curl up into a ball and listen to *Einstein on the Beach* for the next two days, and I knew it. I could feel the urge, the mudslide of depression descending on my bones as I sat by this reporter-at-large human husk. It made me angry that he was almost innocent in his blind privilege.

"No, no, hear me out. You ever been to the Compassion Institute before? It's right down the road from here, and I'd like to take you."

"For what? Old time's sake?" The lights were lowering, and a hush was coming over the crowd. I had all these little absurdly meaningless memories of Mark Drabble: making him toast in the morning before class and him saying wow, thank you, you're the best, and how awful that made me feel because no one who makes toast is ever the best, they are no one's hero. Maybe I could make up for how disappointing I know I was, and am. I also wanted him to shut up and relinquish me from the nauseating feeling of remembering how ill-equipped at caring and loving I was as a teenager.

"Okay, I'll go."

"Lovely!" He pinched my knee with his little claw and turned back around. Then the show began.

* * *

We met the next day under the awning of a refurbished 1930's theater building, because everything in the valley was made to remind us that show business was one of the few interesting shapes reality could take. Mark Drabble took up my fingers and brushed his lips against them, not a kiss, but a light swipe. I recoiled, and he didn't notice.

"I'm so excited you decided to join me here," he said. His face was round and smiley.

I was excited, too—I had fought the unsurmountable weight of life and rage to arrive at this location, far away from my girlhood bedroom. I was surprised and proud. Mark Drabble aside.

"I'm intrigued, I suppose," I shot back. "I feel strangely optimistic."

"You look stunning, my old flame," he said. I could tell that by my using the word optimistic, I had essentially agreed to have sex with him, at least by his calculations. But I was never going to have sex with Mark Drabble, and, honestly, most likely not anyone else ever again. I fished around in the pocket of my coat and handed him a one-hundred-dollar bill.

"That's for keeping your paws off me," I ordered.

"I love that," Mark said, pocketing the money. "I just do."

But when we walked up to the ticket booth, I had to ask for my money right back because it cost exactly one hundred dollars per session at the Compassion Institute. I refused to allow Mark to pay my way, but without the personal payoff the whole date was now open for Mark to interpret in any twisted, erotic way he chose. My shield had been revoked, and I grew wary again.

Through the doorway and into the dim hall, we walked past lotus flower displays and Buddha figurines. Then we entered a waiting room of sorts and sat down in seats. In a few minutes a woman in an assortment of robes delicately walked up to us and asked if we would be having private sessions, or a couples' package.

"Private," I said, just as Mark said, "Couples." She heard "couples" because Mark was a man and therefore louder and more commandeering.

The woman bowed and whispered, "Thank you for choosing the divine way," and shuffled out of the room.

I turned to Mark and said, "I'd prefer to be alone, if we are really doing this kind of transcendental mind game thing."

"Oh, but it's not that, not that at all! We are going to be in a theater and watch movies together. A bonding experience! It will be wonderful," he assured. Before I could protest, or question, the woman came back and guided us to the small theater we would be sharing.

There we watched countless footage reels of human suffering: one humanitarian disaster after another. Flooding; refugee displacement; prison wards; torture victims. We sat together, in that dark and horrible space, for three hours. I would have gotten up and left, except it was fascinating, the pain and horrible suffering. I felt myself become smaller and smaller, a blip, a speck on a mountain, a little bit of dust. What started out in life, then entered the cycle of death, which was relentless, and all enduring. What I had only fathomed as my own fate, became absorbed into the fate of all. The pain on the screen became my own pain, and, joyously, I felt myself feel. No amount of scientific knowledge, nothing I had dreamed about as a genius, could compare to this level of intimacy, the simpatico transfusion of all humanity's entropy into the decay of the whole of me. Their pain was mine. I took it on as my own. I was greedy for it.

But then the lights came on, and there Mark Drabble and I sat, tears streaming down our faces, and the woman in robes entered the room. She held up one hand to gain our attention.

"Now you are feeling pain. You think it is your own. Erroneously, you want it to be yours. But it is not. Picture a rock. Picture a boulder. Picture a flower. Picture a tapestry. These things are you. Put yourself into them. The rock. The boulder. The flower. The tapestry. You absorb all as these objects. You yourself are an object. Absorb. Absorb. Absorb. Now—breathe! Exhale! Exhale all you have inhaled and absorbed. It is love. You are love. All you took in, the pain, was love. You are always love, you are never truly pain. Pain is merely a false option, though unavoidable, because you are, while an object, also human, a fire spirit. You crave pain. You want it. But it gets you nowhere. Humanity is moving forward, one grain of sand at a time. A new era is coming. The era of sand, and rocks, and water: love. You are these elements: love. Give your mind to these elements: love. Offer yourself up. You are nothing more, and nothing less."

The woman, after her speech, bowed as she had when she first met us, and walked silently out of the room.

I was a genius; in youth, I had learned this lesson fast. I looked at Mark, and instead of a man—some distant prick of pain—I saw a rock, I saw a boulder, I saw something that couldn't touch me at all because I had already absorbed all of him, become all of him, and shot out the other side, clean, new, bereft and yet complete—beyond pain and into a world of compassion, which was all love, which was nothing, some version of silence. In merely my first lesson, I had already eaten him with the world. I was powerful.

"That was amazing," I said.

"I thought you would like it." He took my boulder hand. "Come with me to dinner!"

I said no, and then I said, yes, because he couldn't touch me. No one could ever touch me again.

* * *

We dined at a fancy Chinese restaurant down the road, a place reminiscent of the Zoot Suit era and opium dens. We shared dim sum, a sea of what seemed like a thousand steamed dumplings as far as the eye could see. We were all alone and sat opposite one another at a large table, family style.

"I'm a feminist," Mark said. "I find women equal and bewildering. Look at you, you are perfect, my little doll," he said. I had simply stuffed a whole dumpling into my mouth and was chewing ponderously. "Olivia, I found you, and I think I can help you. My heart is large."

I swallowed the dumpling and reached for another. "You already have," I said. "What more could you do?"

Mark leaned forward, elbows on the table, chopsticks poking out of his fingers. "I know a woman, an *extreme* woman, a major donor of the Compassion Institute. I interviewed her for the *Star* last week. She is a *phenome*. I know she's looking for some help with her modeling crew. My heart is so large. Did I say that already?" Mark was patting his chest, as though to make sure it was still there.

I put five dumplings on my small plate and then reached for another and placed it in my mouth, doing the complicated math of calculating how to guarantee that I, not Mark, received the last and best bite of food, which was like playing chess.

"Mark, I am uninterested in joining the shallow and tedious game of the mainstream beauty economy, especially for money."

Mark waved his hands. "Don't worry about that, it's not for money."

I sighed and said, "Listen, Mark, I just graduated, I've got to slow down, and learn how to *get by* in my life. The Compassion Institute was a good start. It really helped me unfeel all my wretched, unwanted feelings of abject futility." I stretched a smile across my face; it was hard, I was tuckered from the cosmic lesson from the day: that nothingness and love were indistinguishable states of being to the universe, and anything but bold neutrality was a cheap lie.

He pushed all the dumplings toward me and said, "Let me help you get your feet on the ground. You need a kick start, someone to lift you up. I have the connection, and I'll make it, because I love you, Olivia, I really do." His eyes were two spinning saucers, black orbs, empty pits. All I saw was a sycophant, a leech, a loser, a blank space. He was mellowing my high of total illumination—I could feel just a bit of it crackling at my edges.

"Who is she?" I asked, "What's her name?"

"You would know her if you saw her. She's at all the charity events in town." I shrugged my shoulders, I hadn't been to any of those, I'd barely left my bedroom.

Mark smiled. "Divya Sasuni," he said. "An actress, a model, a woman currently on several beauty campaigns." He leaned over the table, trying to get closer to me, though we were so far away from each other, and whispered, "Nobody knows which parts of her are real. You'll see what I mean when you meet her."

Divya Sasuni: a name of lore, the name of someone you should know and befriend in this kind of town. And I agreed to meet her because, though I had just seen through the nature of pain and into the root of human existence (a path towards the absence of everyday earthly worries), I knew I was still hampered by my rage and my intellect, my distain for people who just wanted to help me, Mark, professors, all men, the girls I'd gossiped with, centuries of humans, millions of years of our collective waste; I wanted to feel love and nothing, to soulfully know once and for all that the two were one and the same, and when I heard her name, that is what I felt: nothing. I was drawn to that. I was free of care and obstacles. There was me, and there was the abyss.

* * *

When I arrived to Divya Sasuni's property (built into the crags of mountains overlooking the valley of my home), I was struck at first by the area's overt sparseness and vacuity. The house looked like a space station, bland gray concrete smoothed over to remove any impurities or rough edges, and molded into a spherical shape, as though it were a giant egg incubating in the nest of a rock monster's bosom. There was a gravel parking lot with an array of 4x4 Jeeps and Land Rovers, all black and misted over with a fine coat of cosmic material, neither mud nor dirt, but something more naturally reflective, like moon dust. There was no telling how far back the sphere was built into the mountain, but it gave the impression that it was mined deep into the earth's geology. I knocked on the door, a bald eagle screeched, and I waited.

Finally, the heavy front door slid open and a beautiful Asian woman in a crop top and fashionista jeans peered out at me. "Can I help you?" she asked.

"Hello. I'm here for an appointment with Divya Sasuni. For the modelling crew position. We've been emailing," I said. I flashed my diploma and held out a hand for her to shake. She took it cautiously and examined it closely.

"Your cuticles are shredded," she concluded.

I nodded. "I know. I chew them until they bleed. A nervous habit from childhood."

The woman cleared her throat as though embarrassed for me and my childhood, and flipped her long shiny hair back. Then she struck a pose against the doorframe, taking one arm up and leaning in jauntily with her hip cocked out. Her own nails were perfectly manicured, healthy and pink with a clean coating of clear nail polish meant to accentuate her natural glow. "What do you do to your hair? Have you ever tried to relax it?"

It's true that my hair resembled a thicket of vines and thistles.

I mirrored her modeling pose on my side of the stoop, and tried to run my scabby fingers through it, but they got stuck and I had to yank hard to pull myself out. I too tossed my head and shrugged my shoulders. "No," I said. She nodded in agreement, and allowed me inside. As she led me down the cavernous hall, she spoke to me over her shoulder.

"My name is Yoshi-bon, I'm one of Divya's PAs, I handle the workflows in this section of the house, ward one, area blue, if you ever get lost you can look here on the wall and find a map of the grounds, or at least the sections that we are allowed to inhabit. What about you? How old are you? What is your area of expertise? Would you describe yourself as petite? How neutral is your skin tone? How small are your fingers?" I nodded, staring at the rock walls, which were lit by torches of fire. It was cramped and claustrophobic, and felt as though we were descending into a mine. But then, just as I was starting to sweat, the hall-tunnel opened up to a vast chamber of smooth, white stone and marble. The distant sound of rushing water, as if from a waterfall, soothingly played from afar. The soft glow that lit the inner recesses of the house came from an indecipherable source, but was reminiscent of the luminosity given off by a lunar-lit night sky. There was no breeze, or movement, nothing but tranquil time unspooling and spooling back into itself like the slow-pulsing throat of a toad meditating in a creek bed.

I stared up at the ceiling far overhead, a blue and purple diamond kaleidoscope cathedral, and said, "I'm looking for something new." Yoshi-bon flipped her hair and offered me a glass of cucumber water.

"This will help hydrate you so you stop bleeding in odd places. Your lips are very chapped. I recommend Divya's coconut shimmer lipstick in Pearl. Well, this is the foyer, let's go find Divya so you can meet her. She will be interested in what pants size you wear, by the way, and if your breasts are two different shapes. Do you know how to operate heavy machinery? What about small machinery? A digital camera?" I nodded, and Yoshi-bon nodded, too.

We crossed the massive entry way, which was like walking through an entire church, and took a left once we reached the far side. The room we entered next was the color of bone-white wood, unfinished, yet soft. The walls were empty; there was a plush white bed to our right, and to the side of this was a throne made of yet another strange material I was unfamiliar with, something that looked like a large egg cut horizontally down the middle. In its center sat a woman, back erect, legs crossed, long black hair that, if she were to stand, would no doubt have fallen well past her buttocks. Her lips were large, plush fruit pieces, comical, yet beautiful at the same time. Her jaguar eyes were large and open, taking in all that was around her. Her nails were long claws, deep red, on hands that clutched the knee positioned on top of the other in the magnanimous position she was sitting in. Around her own stillness, chaos. A journalist with a recorder's mouthpiece held up to her face; a rack of gowns and garments hovered over by a team of stylists behind her; several squawking babies crawling on their hands and knees in circles; a camera crew; and one little woman who looked like a shorter, rounder double to Divya, holding a fan of one hundred or so one dollar bills, squealing orders and commands at everyone, chasing babies and crew members around, adding more, not less drama to the scene. The reporter was asking his questions:

"And what kind of style would you say this house has been built in?" he wanted to know. He was wearing a fedora and a blazer with the sleeves rolled to his elbows.

Divya nodded and said into the mouthpiece, "Astronautical-inspired minimalist monastery."

"And what kind of materials did you use to build this sanctuary?" the reporter asked in his trained voice.

Divya thought for a moment before saying, "Much of what makes up this home comes directly from the earth. These are the planet's youngest mountains, in my mind making them more open towards the imposition of habitation. We used only what was available, mostly sedimentary and igneous rocks, though there are some metamorphic crags thrown into the mix. The inner chamber floors, doors, and cabinets are made of double-blasted petrified wood, a process that crystalizes the quartz mineralization into a very sturdy, yet calming material that brings me and my family joy and security." She uncrossed her legs and waited patiently for the next question. A baby tried to undo her Egyptian sandal laces, and she picked it off the floor and started bouncing it on her knee. The little woman who I'd seen running in circles appeared from behind the throne and pulled the baby from Divya's lap, whispering sinisterly that Divya was booked for the day, and they'd go find the Bible to read. The journalist's ears perked up at that and he asked, "Would you consider yourselves a religious family?"

Divya nodded again, as though accepting the question into her mind once it made it past several checkpoints.

"We're definitely Christian in our core values. But I find wisdom in many religions, so I would never restrict myself to simply Christianity. Greek mythology is very beautiful to me. So is the Torah. I talk to the Dalai Lama daily, I have his number saved in my phone."

"That's impressive. Would you say you are polytheistic? Many gods over one? Do you believe in reincarnation?"

"I believe in vengeful night demons. I don't know if that answers your question."

"It doesn't, but I'm glad you mentioned it!"

Divya looked up and noticed me standing with Yoshi-bon in the doorway. Before the reporter had a chance to ask for more, Divya stood and walked over to me. I audibly gasped at the full sight of her, a perverse version of perfection, with proportions defying many physics of the female frame. A long, thin neck; a bust like a shelf, each round breast like a ceramic bowl filled to the brim with nectar; a waist as small as any I'd ever seen, as though in a corset, but because her belly was exposed by an oval-shaped gap in the form-fitting dress she was wearing, there wasn't a chance she was wearing one; thighs that expanded far out like a wingspan, and then dropped abruptly just before the knee, in a teardrop. Her skin color was a fair brown, making her of an indecipherable race. She could have been from anywhere, from any nation, from all nations, as though the fate of humanity was simply that she was to be born, and then: she had been.

I felt an array of emotions both new and old—from awe, to desire, to my intellectualized rage. Divya held out her warm hand for me to touch, and I did, I held it in both of mine. "You must be Olivia," she said. "Thank you for coming to meet me. I've heard good things about you from my press team. They say you are a *genius*. I love geniuses. I like to keep them in my orbit. My husband is a genius. He designed this refuge we call home. He lives in the desert six months out of the year, surviving off cactus flesh and visions. I have great respect for your perspective. I'm interested in hearing all about you." She glanced down at my hands which were clinging to her and shaking. She didn't smile once, her face was as plaintive as the Buddha's. I recoiled, strangely frightened of what I'd made contact with, and where I was, apparently a rich man's shaman palace, presided over by a woman-pharaoh, his wife, Cleopatra of outer space, of nowhere, commander of ether. Physical beauty shouldn't matter in this world of indifference. But it does and I became worried.

I realized that the camera crew was at our periphery, fluctuating their borders to get both close-ups and wide-angle shots of our meeting. "I feel like I'm learning so much about you," Divya said, though I had not spoken, and linked her arm through mine. She pulled me through the chamber toward a door at the back of the room. "Let me show you my fit models, as they are the team you would be working with," and when the door opened we entered the pink recesses of a yet another room, adorned with shelves and racks of gowns, shoes, purses, and accessories for as far as I could see. Large ceiling-to-floor mirrors were angled strategically against one side of the room to capture the image of the beholder standing before them. Opaque garments sat one after another on their hangers, daring some thief, some outsider to touch them irreverently—had I ever been so alive? I thought of the Compassion Institute, and I thought of this hole blasted into the side of a mountain.

I turned my head and noticed a long line of female bodies standing rooted and erect atop a pedestal each, motionless and stuck in unique poses. I assumed they were mannequins for their stillness, but then one sneezed and I jumped. "Sorry!" the woman squeaked, and another said, "Bless you," and handed her a hanky pulled from the bust of her flesh-colored spandex bra. Perhaps ten in total, all wearing the same form fitting exercise flesh suit, and suddenly they were all moving, stretching out their limbs. Divya walked over to a light dimmer and turned up the pink illumination so that I would see better. Each woman was exactly Divya's height, and most were her proportions, though one was clearly late in a pregnancy, and another was slightly slimmer than the rest. They all sported the same long black hair as Divya.

"These are my girls," Divya said, "your future crew."

"Are these—you?" I asked. I walked up to one and touched her thigh. She flicked my hand away.

Divya shook her head. "That would be fun! But no, we put out the call for my personal wardrobe fitters last year—based on my measurements. It took *forever* to find the right girls. This one here, you'll see, is a little skinnier, for when I go through my on-again, off-again skinny phase, and this one is eight months pregnant, because I never know when I might be pregnant again, and for some events I like to plan what I'll be wearing a year in advance. It's just nice to be prepared if you can be. I'm in constant communication with my designers, and, let me just say: they are *pissed* if you are pregnant for a gala and they don't have time to prepare. So, what I do is, I pay all my dressers thrice: once for regular me, once for pregnant me, once for skinny me. Because just like being pregnant, I never know when I'm going to be skinny. I exercise three times a day, a total of six hours, but I'm not always dieting. When I do both I get skinny. So, my skinny girl. She's so cute. I *love* them all, such lifesavers! Thank you, ladies!" Divya waved, dimmed the lights, and the women slouched in their silhouettes. I was exhilarated by such rare opulence, and as I shuffled past to follow Divya, one of the women grasped my wrist desperately. "Help me!" she choked. I stole a quick glance into her dim eyes and saw no light, like a broken horse. I was moved.

"What do you think?" Divya asked, as the closet door slammed shut behind us. She was excited and shaking her little fists in the air.

"When do I start?" I asked, churning in the black hole, swept away by its thunder.

* * *

At home, I spoke to Mark on the phone. I had been working for Divya as her wardrobe assistant for three weeks. It paid no money for the first three months (my "trial run"), but was something I could put on my ridiculous resume.

"What do you think?" he asked, making lip smacking noises on the other end of the line. He was eating a popsicle or a lollypop, no doubt. As a weak, small man, treats were things he gave himself regularly.

"I think it's honest work, so for that, Mark, I'll thank you," I said. Unfortunately, I couldn't admit my complete and utter fascination with Divya Sasuni to Mark. Someone like Mark couldn't be trusted with intimate details, nor philosophical musings of the soul. I was sure he'd write a story about it, commodify it, turn it into words, worthless junk, though through it all he kept insisting on how much he loved me, and prized my thoughts.

Well, there was only one way to commodify your life, and that was the Divya Sasuni way—to disconnect from reality so totally that your world no longer resembled the daily grind. I was so appalled by her lifestyle that I'd become obsessed, then enticed, then devoted. I knew I must learn her ways. I'd never have her body, but her peace of mind, I wondered, could it be attained spiritually? I was sure Divya Sasuni was empty in the godly sense. She had everything, so she needed nothing, and in that empty place, there was a lesson to be learned. I'd be her disciple, her second coming. It was the same idea as the Compassion Institute, I thought—emptiness, nothingness, what was the difference? Love was the euphemistic cherry on top.

"I love my fit models so much," Divya often said, and when she said love, she meant accepted, and when she said fit models, she meant herself, for they were her reflections, various hypothetical states of being she did not have to embody if the outfit didn't suit her tastes, her sense of style. She treated them with respect and accommodations, she said, how anyone in their position would want to be treated. She'd made her way up in the industry, she knew what it took to succeed, she had the utmost sympathy.

The fit models, however (my charges), did not agree. In fact, as my devotion for Divya grew, their displeasure with their surroundings expanded. As the first outsider they had seen in years, they thought they'd hatch an escape plan using me as their confidante. They didn't understand however, that I was fighting for the state of my soul, too.

"You know the way out of here," argued Cherry. She'd been working under contract for the team for the last two years. She was, as were all the fit models, miserable. "I haven't seen the sun in years," she said. "I don't care about the money anymore, money is shit." She sniffled as I yanked a vinyl boot up past her knee. "We need help—we wouldn't know the layout at all, they never let us wander beyond our quarters." It was true, the fit models had their own chambers and rock garden. They also had their own kitchen area, and were on surveillance 24/7. I didn't understand what more they could need. Any plan would be fruitless. There was no real place to go. Plus, security would be a nightmare; you never saw them anywhere, which just made me more paranoid, and I assumed it was a high-tech gorilla-style outfit.

"Listen," I said loudly for all to hear. It was safe to have a frank conversation since Divya arrived only after the models were fitted. "I don't know what you think you'll gain by leaving this place. Out there it's a wasteland."

"I'm so sick of this artificial light, I could scream," another said. I looked at them lined up, displayed and gorgeous in the pink light and chic outfits I'd just fitted them into. They made $200 a day and sent it all home to their families, like peasants. They didn't need the money here, for all their physical needs were met: shelter, medicine, food, clothing. And yet they insisted on the human connection. As a result, they lived unfree and shackled, they said, all on contracts that extended well beyond what they now believed they could handle. They said they were going insane.

"You're not going to get what you want from that world out there," I consoled, for I had authority in this area. Like Plato's philosopher who escaped the cave of fire to see the world for what it was, I had an updated message for the captives: "Outside the cave, inside the cave, it's exactly the same. Except outside the cave is worse." The world of shadows was superior, in my honest opinion. More importantly, I couldn't help them because then I'd be out of both something to do and my spiritual security.

Tina, the pregnant one, burst into sobs. She was mercurial, a week away from her due date. "What about my baby?" she wept. "What will they do with it?"

"The baby will be fine!" I said. Obviously, they'd just add it to the litter of other babies roaming the premises, lots of nannies, lots of attention from Divya's sister, the short, fat version of Divya, who would take it under her wing, feed it all the right formulas and supplements. In fact, Divya was working on a recipe of baby formula for the commercial market that she swore by: Baby-Baby, the formula that nourished the baby inside the baby, the perpetual baby in us all, our tether to the world beyond our own, from where we all came, and to where we all returned. The product was a collaboration with her husband, the desert shaman. They texted one another often about the developing concept, and the release date. It would be ready for Tina's baby, I was sure. I told her so.

"That's not the point," Tina cried. "It's not natural, how did I even end up here?"

That I couldn't answer. I'd assumed they'd all been down on their luck strippers of the valley, but didn't pry. It didn't matter, and I didn't want to know. If it was a scheme they'd fallen victim to, I was jealous. How many of the preyed upon hit the jackpot? It was a loophole they couldn't appreciate. They were fools for wanting frivolous freedom. I told them that.

Divya arrived with an assistant and looked critically at the assembly before her, the vessels to her vessel, each gown a rubber glove that accentuated their natural curves. If the world was a game, you could play it very well. Divya was graceful. She didn't care about what she cared about. It could all burn up in a fire, and she'd simply walk away, unscorched, pristine, ageless, atomic particles making way like the Red Sea.

* * *

I met the genius shaman, a man named Ralph, one day on my way to the bathroom. He was sitting at a harpsicord, playing rapidly. He wore a backwards baseball cap, a puffy bomber jacket, slacks, and slippers. His lips were dried and crusted, parched from the desert. I waited for him to finish his number, before approaching with a glass of cucumber water and introducing myself.

"Olivia Park," I said, holding out my hand. "Wardrobe assistant of the fourth ward."

He stared at my hand blankly, as though unaware of the custom. I pushed it toward him further, encouraging him to take it, until he seemed offended or scared, and flipped my hand away with his shoulder. He commenced his playing.

When I returned to the fitting room I told the girls about the meeting. They groaned and gagged.

"That man is a disaster," said Cherry. "When he's home, he comes in here soliciting strange offers that he pretends aren't sex. He's a drunkard who claims he is a spiritual beneficiary. Totally unoriginal."

"Divya believes he's a genius," I said, though I agreed that money had a tendency to regress men, and though I'd witnessed him playing the harpsicord with otherworldly talent, it had been like watching a troglodyte do the same: as amazing as it was unsettling.

"He's a richie who rides the coattails," said Cherry. "God*damn* I wish I had a cigarette." The models now filled their empty hours sharing fantasies of all the mischief they would get into once they escaped, which itself was a fantasy: running down the mountain in their bare feet to smoke cigarettes at brunch on a patio by the ocean, stuffing themselves with French toast and mimosas until four in the afternoon. Then a siesta in the sand, then their families. For their daughters they would bare gifts of gowns, stolen from Divya's fashion archives, and for their sons and husbands, aged whiskey from the mountain vaults, and they'd drink and laugh until the sun went down and came up again. I tried to let these stories wash over me with no lingering effect, but, unfortunately, the day sounded nice and therapeutic.

I was wearing my vision magnifiers, painting individual Starry Nights on each of the models' nails (Divya's orders, as she'd just had her own nails done in this style), when Tina's water broke.

"Ahhh!" she screamed, the liquid sloshing across her pedestal. "My baby! My baby! My baby!"

The closet door flung open and Ralph marched in, a team of lab coats behind him. One of the coats escorted Tina away, while Ralph and the others used long swabs to scoop the liquid into small vials and plastic ziplock bags. When finished, the coats marched away and Ralph turned around and said, "Ladies." He gave a little bow and left.

"That motherfucker is crazy," said Cherry. "I hope he gets killed in a rock slide."

"Or stung to death by a scorpion," said another.

"Or eaten by a mountain lion," said another.

"Or picked apart by vultures in a meditative trance," I said, before I could stop myself. The women all stared, and I blushed.

* * *

At a business meeting with Divya I broached the subject of Tina returning to work, and the outcome of the birth. Divya excused everyone but me from around the large, shiny table and stared at me very seriously.

"Tina has been let go. But the baby turned out healthy and beautiful." Her stern face melted and she smiled sweetly. "She looks just like me."

"Oh, really? You fired Tina? Because you're right, she looked just like you, even pregnant."

"No, not Tina, the baby. She looks just like me."

"Ah. I see. Well, it must be hard to have to let that one go…" It was true that Divya was obsessed with her appearance and beautiful babies, hence the commercial line of beautifying baby formulas.

"I didn't let the baby go. That baby is mine," she said. She pulled out her phone and showed me all the pictures she'd taken of the two of them together, how she loved that baby like she loved herself: unconditionally.

I signed very loudly. This turn of events was unfortunate. I knew Tina would be devastated, clambering at the mountain, trying to claw her way back in. It was not the way I wanted Tina to be. It was not the way I'd hoped the pregnancy would turn out.

Divya put her phone away and told me to take notes. She dictated that it was my job to find Tina's replacement, giving me her measurements.

"But why not hire Tina back? She's already perfect," I said.

Divya said no. Tina was no longer pregnant. We needed a pregnant model. She already had enough "regular" models in her wardrobe. I told her I'd do my best, and she grabbed me by the throat and said that wouldn't be good enough.

In the bathroom, I stared at the handprint wrung around my neck. It was perfectly sized and shaped—even the claw marks left little bits of gold embedded in my flesh, flecked off from the nails that had been freshly painted earlier that day.

* * *

I took my little bit of lunch down by the reflecting pool in the foyer of the cave and stared at my myself. The chef had given me what he gave me most days: kabocha squash and a cup of tea. It was for my nails and hair. Divya believed that you created beauty from the inside out, meaning, from what you put into your intestines and eventually shat out. I ate my bit of squash and sipped my tea; it all tasted like ash. My plan had not been going according to plan ever since Divya revealed that she had stolen Tina's baby and then fired her. The calmness I had sensed emanating from her that first day, I realized, was simply the steady resolve of someone willing to plow through life the way they had plowed through the earth. Her tenacity to live on her own terms, so secluded, was the fear of being held accountable for her actions. I was disgusted with myself, to have become the acolyte of someone so consumed with such common human folly.

* * *

I attended the Compassion Institute that night, dispensing of one hundred dollars that I hadn't yet made at work. I sighed as I pushed the bill across the counter. Somehow, I'd grown weary, and not in the way that a genius does—it was totally different. I was a failure, as my plans to be filled with the nothingness of love had failed; I was filled with everything else that comes along with feeling anything: hope, fear, desire, and revenge. I asked for a solo theater to purge my soul.

The robed woman from last time set me up in a private theater, and I watched home videos of a family growing up in a house in a nearby wholesome town. As the children aged into their teen years, I became happy and attached, learning their names, favorite foods and subjects in school. The final reel of film showed their house burning to the ground in a statewide wildfire, claiming the lives of many, including the family. The footage left the question open, but it was heavily insinuated. I thought of Tina's baby, and I thought about Tina. I thought about the other women.

Through the tears in my eyes that blurred my vision, I pulled out my laminated diploma and tried to read it: Olivia Park, Bachelor and Philosopher of the Arts. All those years in school, learning to think not for myself, but of myself. The only way to redemption was to go out in a blaze.

* * *

I hustled up the mountain in a ski mask and black body suit. When I reached the front door to the cave, I used my stiff, laminated diploma to shimmy the rock lock open. If I ran into anybody, I'd tell them that I'd left my purse on the premises, in the fit-model quarters. I slipped inside and saw Yoshi-bon slumped and sleeping at her post by the front door. She snored herself awake and I diligently recited the purse line. She must have dreamed that she had let me in, because she just nodded and led me through the torch-lined halls; I memorized every turn we took. As we approached the quarters I said, "Yoshi-bon, when we get to the room, do you mind leaving to go take a picture of Tina's baby to send me on my phone? I would be very grateful. I love a good, beautiful baby." Yoshi-bon yawned deeply and said, "Okay." She was sleepwalking now. I looked into her dim eyes. There was nothing there.

At the bedroom door, I said, "Yoshi-bon: go to the baby quarters and take a picture of Tina's baby." She wandered away, and I opened the door before me. I didn't give a thought about security. How could I?

"Hello," I whispered, "Hello! Wake up!"

The models stretched. Their limbs moved like the sea. Even in the middle of the night, the lights were pink and kept at a low, dim level. They wore eye masks to block it out, and as they pulled the masks up, one by one, I lifted my own.

"Oliva," said Cherry, "it's you."

"Let's go," I said. "Follow me!"

There was no time to grab anything, because in the end there was nothing to grab. They left as they were, in the flesh-colored body suits. We ran the corridors, me leading the way, afraid to look back.

When we emerged from the cave, the dawn's sun was cresting the mountain, and in the new light, beyond the pale pink fabrication, I saw the unique shapes each woman made, both before and against the rocks. Their shadows, they waved as if before fire, and mine too, a stream of silhouettes rushing me, as I moved with the women toward water.

THICK CITY

/ Katie Jean Shinkle

Meanwhile, what does she taste like after all? More than mint & calendula & nasturtiums & lavender in November fog, the kind that reminds you of movies set in England or swimming under the cobble-pebble lake trestle?

Her taste on your lips. You are intimately aware of what she does, and how she does it. She is, after all, your very favorite. But then, there are those times. "Why do you always act surprised?" she says. Here, you want to jump through the screen, strangle the sweaty, hairy man with the tinted sunglasses. He's the one who puts his hands down the front of her shirt first, and at 28:12 is from behind initiating a scene that at 43:57 ends with a double money shot down the curves of her waist. These videos inspire love, and envy in you. You want to pull her off the leather couch, tell all those people they don't deserve her.

She is a star at Dangling Willy's. She transforms into VERONICA!!! the voice echoes into a computer application that makes it twang. Hair extensions, false eye lashes, contouring, nipple pasties, the waves of creation. VERONICA!!! dances only to Master P, DMX, and Montell Jordan in rotation and exclusively. On your birthday, you get her to dance, "to the biggest cliché of her life" she says, a Nine Inch Nails song, fulfilling a pathetic teenage fantasy from 1994.

And while you are in love, you wait until she is asleep to talk to the Other: "Sir." you whisper into your phone, "What will you feed me off of: Fiesta dinnerware, Marigold and Scarlet." Sir doesn't want to hear about your pedestrian Fiesta dinnerware fantasies. "Take your clothes off," Sir says.

Even over the phone, you comply. You obey.

The next day, you wake late in the afternoon. VERONICA!!! has gone to work. You have many missed calls. Sir is reciting esoteric poetry. This is how you both communicate your wants and needs.

Through lines you recall things that are unsafe to tell other people, relay moments that have defined you, moments you carry in your heart: once, at the absolute peak of loneliness, before VERONI-CA!!!, before Sir, you let two men you met from the Internet spit on and hit you, make you crawl during sex (which is what you wanted), and after the hook-up, for which you paid, you went to the mall to buy cologne. How some teenagers were driving erratically in front of you, so you laid on your horn. How when you finally parked, they circled the lot until you got out of your car. How they yelled, "Fuck you, fat ass faggot!" How you never entered the mall. How you went home and stared at a wall for an hour. You didn't leave your house for another week.

Once you get home from walking around the city, from throwing your phone in a garbage can uptown, VERONICA!!! is asleep in the king-size bed tucked neatly under a nude painting of herself. Before you threw your phone away, you wrote to Sir *let's meet, please, we must, or I'll die*. You couldn't bring yourself to go through with it. You walked right past his building as he watched you from the window.

THICK CITY

/ Katie Jean Shinkle

Meanwhile, Annie and the telephone bill are driving across town to retrieve her daughter from soccer practice, top speed, screeching tires. She doesn't turn her headlights on. She parks and stands at the edge of the field, watching girls with short legs kick and follow a ball tired, as if in slow motion. There is a whistle, the coach yells, "That's a wrap!" Her daughter, Evie, and Evie's long, swishing ponytail find her in the crowd. Evie grabs her warm-up jacket and her Bible from the bench, and she follows her at a distance back to the car.

During the car ride home, they both are silent, listening to local public radio. Annie so tired of this Bible thing, Evie's father gifting her one last month. Annie is completely against it. Their daughter is too young to consider such things, she'll come to it when she's older. But, older is now, I guess. Evie taps her fingers haphazardly on the red leather cover of the Bible, and the sound overrides the voices in the speakers, in her head. "Enough," she says to her, and Evie looks hurt in a way Annie wasn't expecting.

Back at home, pitch dark, but still very early evening. Annie looks out to the backyard and sees Evie as a little girl, not even ten years old. She is rubbing up against a tree, the trunk's bark between her legs. She is wearing hot pink stirrup pants. Luckily, Evie has hyper-sensitive hearing. She can hear anyone coming for her from any direction. Snap of branch, stop the heaving. Rustle of leaves, cease the gyration. She remembers feeling a mix of relief and terror: Where did Evie learn that motion? Did she find her XXX videos? Walk in on her unnoticed? Of course not, children figure out pleasure, explore their bodies freely. Annie decided then and there to not embarrass or shame, to talk frank using science, facts, but she never did. She doesn't like confrontation.

Annie and Evie's ponytail are eating soggy peas, leftover steak, sticky bread. No complaints from either of them. The telephone bill is on the table between them. Annie clears her throat and imagines a scenario where she confronts her about it, screaming and swearing and name calling until she is bulging in the neck. Bulging in the neck from yelling is the worst thing she can imagine.

Annie has another memory: at the doorway of her pink bedroom, Evie is tearing through an encyclopedia, ripping the edges of pages, she can still see the figures of the circulatory system, the muscles shiny, outlined in silver. Annie says, "What are you doing, Evie?" and Evie says "Penis, Ma, I am looking for penis, it was here a few minutes ago and now it's gone. Where is the penis, Ma?" Annie laughs. She was five years old.

The reality is, she thinks, as she spills a spoonful of peas onto the floor, missing her mouth, that she could never say something like that to this beautiful, gangly, young girl with her high blonde ponytail, her gap between her teeth. How can you look at a gap like that, passed down from her father's mother's side, and blame anything on it? You can't, Annie thinks. You cannot do it.

Evie swirls her food around her plate. She looks bored. She grabs the bill. Annie freezes, tries not to make eye contact, can't seem to make her mouth or her hands work. If she could, she would snatch the bill from her hands, tear it to pieces and throw them at her, watch them land on her late, crappy dinner. Accuse her. Punish her. Annie is not the one who called these numbers.

"Ma, are these 1-900 numbers? Like in the back of *Rolling Stone*? The ads with the girls with big boobs? Isn't that illegal?"

Annie can feel the heat rising from somewhere in her chest, into her neck, through her jaw that feels like it is ripping through the skin of her face. She meets Evie's big eyes colored full of disappointment.

"Ma, we need to talk." She folds her hands on her lap. "Do you know Jesus Christ as your Lord and Personal Savior?" she asks. "Do you want to?"

THICK CITY

/ Katie Jean Shinkle

Meanwhile, Coley uses the sun visor's mirror to watch herself brush her long, wavy, lettuce hair and scoops it into a topknot salad, the messier the best. She is finicky about how much the ends look tossed precisely so. A spectacle of prepackaged manufacturing, yet it has to look organic. She pushes up her fly-aways, uses licked fingers to force baby hairs to stand on end. Must look exerted. Natural. No effort, all effort.

She slaps the sun visor up, sits in dawn twilight, adjusts the ring light behind her which gives the illusion that her cheekbones are more angular so she doesn't have to suck in as much, purse her lips as often.

A few minutes before, she opened her throat and slammed down to the top of the label a 2-liter of Coca-Cola and then slowly replaced the liquid with a half-pint of Jonnie Walker Black. She loves watching the golden liquid coat the inside of the plastic, rounding every curve of the bottle like a wave. A loud screeching outside of the car makes her jump and her thighs involuntarily squeeze the newly full, uncapped 2-liter between them, spewing booze and soda all over her leggings, her car seat, her steering wheel. She doesn't react much beyond a cringe. She takes a long drink from the bottle to compose herself, suckling the ridged top with her lips, running her tongue mindlessly inside the smoothness of the corrugated opening. The world at this hour is horizon-full and almost shadow empty. She only has a short window of time before the sun will be fully up and her own natural movie set will vanish.

There is a kind of geometry to this light, she thinks, when the gradations feel rapturous, all encompassing. Like when Mr. Schwinn drew on the board in middle school art class to teach about shading and dimension. She felt like she could live inside of his drawings and stay there, in the light and depth, down the streets and in the mansions which were better and bigger than where any of them lived.

She remembered, then, how she had convinced everyone in that class she was rich and lived in a house with ten bathrooms. Nina D., who lived next door, thank god, went along with her lies, though later blackmailed her. As payment to keep her secret, Nina made Coley call her on Saturday morning for "beauty tips," saying she needed them. Nina lived for adoration, but rarely received it. But when Coley called, Nina just told her to drink more water, which wasn't bad advice, considering, but certainly not the beauty tip she was hoping to hear. Coley wanted Nina's secret map of how desire worked, the ways in which she could hold it in her hands and mold it, draw point A to B and go there, live in the sprawling gardens of the neighborhoods she shaded in. The light outside roils along the tops of the trees, threatens to burst through in oranges and pinks at any minute. She's losing her moment.

Coley dips a handkerchief into the whiskey and Coke, soaks it, and puts the handkerchief to her forehead, to the back of her neck, to her collar bone. She soaks the handkerchief and dabs her hair. She squeezes the brown, sticky liquid underneath her armpits, squeezes it above her sports bra and runner's tank top of the same material. Everything must look damp, she must have beads of moisture in some places, and pools of moisture in other places. She must look like she sweated hard, but not so hard as to be unpleasant.

She wrings out more liquid onto the bottom of her tank top. There is almost too much light, so she has to hurry. She takes out her phone and starts the video. "Hey Team Let's Do It! What a great day! Rise and Shine! Smashed my workout, and oh babes, I feel soooo good! I didn't want to come in today, I wasn't feeling it, wanted to stay in bed! But wow, I'm so glad I got to the gym and worked those feelings alllll the way out! Remember: No one is going to clap for you, you have to clap for your own damn self! Show up and try! Never give up! Do it for you and no one else! You got this! Don't forget today is the last day for 25% off my customized fitness plan with code LETSDOIT. Love you!"

Her phone clicks to indicate the video has stopped, she uploads to her feed, her story, and closes the app. She takes slug after slug from the 2-liter, closes her eyes, imagines God breastfeeding her, huge hands nestle and cradle. She finally takes a breath, wipes her mouth on her forearm, opens the window, and dumps the rest out, splashing her car door. She throws the bottle on the ground, rolls her window ¾ of the way up. The world is in full-on morning. She is almost in a full-on panic. She lights the bottom of a small, bulbous, glass pipe, sucks and exhales thick yellow smoke which mostly fills the car, but also leaks languidly into the air outside. She leans her head on the steering wheel, sets the pipe in her cupholder. The notifications pile up: red hearts and hashtags, a chorus of agreement, #girlswhodieforhealth, #bodybaggoals, #deathmotivation, #extremelifeloss, #shecroaks, which rise from her phone's screen out-of-focus and dropping. She lights a cigarette, the gas station's neon Laguintas beer sign is all fritz and blink. Beyond the sign, inside the gas station, the young man behind the counter smiles while counting money from the drawer. Almost shift change. Miguel, he's practically a friend at this point. Here is everything she knows about him: He is working on his degree in materials science and engineering at the university downtown, lives at home to cut costs even though his parents have said they will pay for housing. He likes living at home. Still has a brother in high school, and they are close. He likes his family. He likes the gas station. He likes his classes. He's a very good student. He's going to be a very good engineer. Here is everything he knows about her: Nothing. She watches him run his fingers through his swoopy bangs in flirtation at a customer she cannot see, this time the creases around his mouth look concerned, in an ohhh instead of an ahhhh. She stubs her cigarette out into the cupholder. She doesn't even attempt to slice the smoke with her hand to clear it.

Her clothes are dry, it happened so quickly. Her face, is too, for the most part, except her dirty scalp and shredded lettuce tendrils, which are wilted and rotten. She takes a giant bite from a king-sized Kit Kat she always buys from Miguel before she makes her daily workout video, her only meal of the day. The chocolate tastes like chemicals on her tongue. She has a moment of clarity—all the candy in the gas station is poison, the government is poisoning us— and spits the mouthful on the floor mat. She regrets throwing the whiskey away. When she backs her car out, she hears the plastic bottle crush underneath the tires.

NO MEASURE

/ Kelly Krumrie

Weather expands the desert. Sand blows into the city. New grass locks it to the ground. The quarry dislodges rock. Sand is collected and melted into glass. Glass around the buildings, glass that responds to heat, glass in the control room, the computer screen, glass in front of your eye. From sand in the desert, rock in the quarry, grass in strict rows—all documented, all contained in a valley until sent out. I imagine this valley. You and I are here. Records, matter slipping through my fingers. The scale of the landscape hard to grasp. I am deceived by the nearness of things and by their remotenesses. I am being explicit. It is no matter. We're of no measure. My mind's eye, my attention, parts grasses to find your hands, parts grasses to find your hands. Make an appearance; show me a further study. If I keep writing *glass* I can see what it's made of. Each procedure in this place a transformation or an extraction. Your remoteness—I want to be pulled out into.

There is a break in the volume and mass—a disintegration of forces. I am deceived by remotenesses. Today you walk the perimeter with your notebook and pencil, pausing to count and record, stopping to look up at the sun, holding up your hand to block it.

There are always new instruments. I thread things together.

My walk through the landscape bends back the grass blades or I leave no trace.

The distance measured behind glass, after the fact, later, we look out the window, and the tread on each row is in line, a tight fiber.

Attention shapes matter. See, I hold the point between distance and proximity over and over. Now I have it in my grasp. I perceive the nearness of things and their remotenesses. Your remoteness is like a mirror, and these perceptions are each points that I mirror and am pulled into.

My eye's reach's locations. My hand's course is like my eye's. My hand is here, and here. My sight bends back.

Arrest occurs between the actual and the possible. A point splits my vision and I see the desert all at once this instant.

When I leave the edge of my imagination, slope has no measure. There is ground here, sand and grass. Your hip: I trail my finger along it.

Is your shape imperceptible? Or just beyond the threshold? Or at it?

The map shapes the perceptibility of the territory, its imagined tractability. In my imagination, I put my hand out. An unknown event is a synthetic operation. It's when I put my hand out. I see it for an instant. I attend to the perceptible and to what I can't know.

An imagination shapes the territory my hand crosses. My attention to my own hand, its crosses. Pull me to

Duration, labor, mark, could

We lie collinear.

What is real is the form that is materialized. I seek a perceptual limit. To view it otherwise than with the eye.

The fence line is hours long, you say, it's like a chemical, this boundary, in that it reacts. You hold up a piece of glass.

Tell, computation, given, hold

THE SEARCH FOR INTELLIGENT LIFE

/ Tetman Callis

I have
   I've been
   I have and I've been more than three or three or two or four today, yet I have never found any such interesting item like yours. You've got the
   You have the definite item it's, it's, it is, that is, pretty well worth enough for me.

                              #

In my opinion
   that is, personally, in my view, if all you people
   people like you, like I like you, if you
   all of you, or more of you, made as good a definite item as you did, the one you did, this would be or will be a much more
   much more, a lot more useful than ever before place.
   Place
   this place, I couldn't or could not resist or refrain from telling you, like I like you. Very well. Perfectly. Perfectly well. You. Exceptionally well.
   It is written! I will
   I'll
   right away, immediately, take hold of, grab, clutch, grasp, seize, snatch, as I can not
   can't
   in finding, or find, to find your
   Do you have, that is, you've any? Please. Kindly allow, permit, let me realize, recognize, understand, know, so that in order that I may, just may, just could, subscribe my thanks. It is
   It's appropriate, perfect, the best time to make some plans for the future and it is, it's time to be happy. I have, I've read this and if I could, I want to wish to desire to suggest to you a few
   some

interesting things.

Perhaps

Maybe you could or can. I want to wish to desire more, even more things! It is, It's appropriate, perfect, the best time to make a few or some plans for the future, the longer term, the long run, and it is, it's time to be happy. I have, I've learned this, I've put up, and if I may, just may, could I want to wish to desire to suggest, recommend, or counsel you about some interesting fascinating attention-grabbings?

Perhaps

Maybe you could, or can, have the next subsequent items relating to, referring to, regarding this. I want to wish to desire to learn more, even more things approximately about it! I have, I've been more than, greater than, three threes these days. Nowadays, today, lately as of late, yet but

I never by no means found or discovered any interesting fascinating attention-grabbings like yours. It's

It is lovely, pretty beautiful, worth value and of price enough for me. In my opinion. Personally. In my view, if all the people like you, and I like you, made just the right good excellent items as you did (you probably did), this place will be, shall be, might be, will probably be, can be, will likely be, much more or a lot more useful than ever before.

Aha! It's a nice pleasant good fastidious discussion conversant dialogue, concerning the item, here at this place, now at this time, it's me also here at this place. I am sure this has touched all people visitors, it's a really really nice, pleasant, good and fastidious item piece. Wow, and this item piece is nice, pleasant, good, or fastidious, and my sister, younger sister, is analyzing such as these kinds of things, so thusly therefore I am going to tell and inform and let her know of this conveyance. Saved! I really like

I like

I love your Way cool! Very extremely valid! I appreciate you and this and the

and also

plus the rest of the also very extremely, very also really really good. Hi, I do believe I do think this is an excellent item, this stumbledupon item. I will, I am going to, I'm going to, I may come back or return or revisit once again here yet.

#

Money and freedom! Is the best! The greatest way! To change, may you be rich and continue. Woah! I'm really loving or enjoying digging this.

#

It's simple, yet effective. A lot of times it's very hard, very difficult, challenging, tough, and hard to get that perfect balance between superb usability, user friendliness usability, and visually apparent visual appeal appearance. I must say that you've
you have
you've done an awesomely amazing and very good or superbly fantastic excellent great job with this. In addition
Additionally
Also, Superb Exceptional Outstanding Excellent!
These are really actually in fact truly genuinely great enormously impressive wonderful fantastic ideas in regarding the concerning item. You have touched some nice or pleasantly good fastidious points and factors here. Anyway, keep up. I love, I really like, I enjoy, I like
Everyone loves what you guys are usually tending to be up to. This sort of
This type of Such.
This kind of clever work and exposure! Keep up the superb, terrific, very good, greatly good, awesome, fantastic, excellent, amazing, wonderful
works
guys
I've incorporated or added or included you guys.

#

Howdy
Hi there
Hey there
Hi Hello Hey!
Someone shared this so I came to give it a

look look

it over take a look check it out. I'm definitely enjoying loving, and will be! Terrific Wonderful Great Fantastic Outstanding Exceptional Superb Excellence, and wonderful terrific brilliant amazing great excellent fantastic outstanding superb style and design.

I love that I really like

I enjoy

I like

Everyone loves what you guys are usually tending to be up to. This sort of type of Such. This kind of clever work! Keep up the superb, terrific, very good, greatly good, awesomely fantastic, excellently amazing wonderful works, guys, I've incorporated or added and included

Howdy Hi there, Hey there, Hi Hello Hey, would you mind stating which you're with?

#

I'm looking on planning to be going to start my own in the near future soon, but I'm having a tough or difficult hard time making a decision. Selecting choosing, or deciding between the two or three or four. The reason I ask is because

I had to ask! Howdy Hi there.

Hi Hey there

Hello Hey would you mind letting me know? I must say, can you suggest recommending an honest and reasonably fair price?

#

Thanks a lot, Kudos. Cheers. Thank you. Many thanks.

Thanks, I appreciate it!

I love,

I really like,

I like, like everyone loves it when people, when individuals, when folks, whenever people, like you, I like people like you, come together to get together and share. Keep it up and continue the good work to stick with it!

It, in fact, was an amusement on account of it. Look in advance to far more added! By the way

However, how can or could we communicate? Howdy Hi there, Hey there, Hello Hey, just wanted to give you a quick head. The item seems to be running off. I'm not sure if this is an issue or something to do, but I thought I'd figure to let you know. They look great though! Hope you get the problem issue solved or resolved or fixed soon. Kudos Cheers Many thanks and Thanks.

This is a topic that is that's, which is close to near to my heart... Cheers. Many thanks. Best wishes. Take care. Thank you! Where Exactly

where are your details though?

It's very easy, simply trouble-free, straightforward, effortless to find out I'm having a tough time but, I'd like to send or shoot you, an e-mail email. I've got some you might be interested in hearing.

Either way, great, and I look forward to seeing it grow over time. Hola Hey there Hi Hello Greetings! I've time now and finally got the bravery courage to go ahead and give you a shout out from New Caney Kingwood Huffman Porter Houston Dallas Austin Lubbock Humble Atascocita Tx Texas! Just wanted to tell you, mention, say Greetings from Idaho Carolina Ohio Colorado Florida Los Angeles California! I'm bored to tears bored to death bored at work so I decided during lunch break I enjoy really liking the love present provided here, and can't wait to take a look when I get home. I'm shocked amazed and surprised. It's like you, and I like you, such as you read my learned mind's thoughts!

#

You seem to appear to understand to know how to grasp so much a lot

approximately

about this, like you, such as

you wrote the book in it or

something. I think I feel, I believe, that you—that you, simply that you—just could or can do with some few to force pressure and drive power, getting the message house at home a bit, a little bit, however,

but other than instead of that, this is that, and is great, is wonderful, fantastic, magnificent.

I'll

I will definitely
certainly be back. I visited multiples of many several various
varieties but except however, the quality feature currently present
and existing is really actually in fact, truly genuinely marvelous,
wonderful, excellent, fabulous, and superb.

#

Howdy Hi there Hi Hello, from time to time I own a similar one and
I was just wondering, curious if you get a lot and if so
If so, how do you prevent or reduce or stop to protect against it,
any anything you can advise to suggest or recommend? I get so much
lately it's driving me madly insane or crazy, so any assistance or help
or support is very much appreciated.

#

Greetings! Very helpful
Very useful advice within!
It is the
It's the little changes that make
which will make
that produce
that will make the biggest
the largest
the greatest
the most important
the most significant Many thanks!
I really truly seriously absolutely love your
Very nice Excellent Pleasant Great colors. Did you create your-
self? Please reply back as I'm looking to trying, to planning, to
wanting, to hoping, to attempting, my own
my very own
and would like to want, would love to know, to learn and find
out where you got or what the
exactly what the
just what the
Thanks. Many thanks. Thank you. Cheers. Appreciate it. Kudos!
Hi there! Hello there! Howdy! This item couldn't

could not
be any better much better! Thank you for Thanks for Many
thanks for, I do appreciate you! Wow, Whoa, Incredibly Amazing!
This looks exactly just like my old one!

#

Excellent Wonderful Great Outstanding Superb choice!
There is
There's definitely certainly a lot to a great deal to know about,
learn about, find out about. I like
I love
I really like all the all of the points.
You made
You've made
You have made some decent good
really good
to find out more, to learn more, and found most individuals and
most people will go along on this.
Hi Hello Hi there What's up every week on a regular basis.

#

You're awesome, keep doing what you're doing up the good work
it up! I simply just could not, couldn't leave or depart or go away
before suggesting that I really extremely actually enjoyed and loved
the standard usual person, an individual who supplies or provides
for your or on your or in your or to your guests? I'm going to gonna
be back again frequently, regularly, incessantly, steadily, ceaselessly,
often continuously, in order to check up on and check out, inspect,
investigate, and cross-check. I wanted what I needed, what I want
to I need, to thank you for this greatly excellent and fantastically
wonderful very good every little bit of bit of it!!
I have what I've got, I have got you to look at.

#

Hi Hello Hi there What's up, just wanted to mention or, say, tell you
what, I enjoyed liking and loved this. It was inspiring, funny, practi-

cally helpful. Keep on! I leave a drop to create, leave a drop each time when whenever. I appreciate, like especially, enjoying if I have something. It is
Usually it is
Usually it's
It's a result of triggered passion, the fire of sincerity displayed.

#

And on and on, after this. Still doing what they can. I was actually moved I was, was actually excited enough to drop leaves, drop and write, create a thought, a comment, a response. I do have
actually do have some
a few
questions a couple of questions
2 questions for you if you don't
do not usually
do not tend not to mind, if it's all right, okay? Is it
Could it be just only simply me, or does it seem to appear or give the impression
look
look as if
look like some or a few of these, look or appear or come across like they are
as if they
are like coming from dead individuals?

#

I'd, I would, like to keep up. Could you would you make a list? Hi there Hello, I enjoy all. I like, wanted to support you. I always, constantly, every time, spent my half, daily, every day, all the time along with a cup or mug of coffee. I always, for all time, all the time, constantly, every time, because, since as for the reason that
then after that
trying to persuade or convince me. I have always disliked the idea because of the expenses and costs. I've been about a year, and am nervous, anxious, worried, concerned about fantastic, very good, and excellently great good things. Is there a way I can? Any

kind of
Any help would be really greatly appreciated!

#

Hello Hi, Hello there Hi there, Howdy, Good day! I could have
sworn I've been before, but after looking at some
a few of the many, I realize it's new to me. Anyways
Anyhow
Nonetheless
Regardless, I'm definitely certainly happy, pleased, or delighted
I found that I discovered, I came across
I stumbled upon it frequently, regularly, and often! Terrific
Great Wonderful! This is
That is the type of the kind of that are meant to
that are supposed to
that should be shared around the
across the Disgrace. Shame on the now not not, no longer this
up upper higher! Come on over and talk over with, discuss with,
seek advice from, visit, consult. Thank you. Heya I'm
I am for the first time here. I came across and I find it truly re-
ally useful & it helped me out a lot much. I hope to give something
back and help to aid others like you helped to aid me.

#

Hi Hello, Hi there, Hello there Howdy, Greetings, I think I believe
I do believe I do think.
There's no doubt.
When I
Whenever I look
take a look
it looks fine but
when however, when however, if however, when I just, I simply,
I merely wanted to give you
provide you with a quick head! Other than that
Apart from that
Besides that Aside from
that, fantastically wonderful great excellence! A person, Some-

one Somebody, necessarily and essentially lends a hand to help assist, seriously, critically, significantly, severely I might state. This is
That is the first
very first time and to this point so far, thus far up to now? I'm amazed and surprised.
Great Wonderful Fantastic Magnificent Excellent!
Heya I'm
I am for the primary, the first time here. I came across, found this, and I am finding this find to find it truly a really useful & helpful find, & it helped me out a lot much. I am hoping
I hope I'm hoping
to give, to offer, to provide, to present something
one thing back again
and help aid others like you, such as you helped and aided me.

#

Hello Hi, Hello there, Hi there, Howdy Good day, Hey there! I just
I simply would like to or want to wish to give you a huge big thumbs up for your great excellent
you've got
you have got
here right here. I will be
I'll be
I am coming back to returning for more soon. I'm always all the time, every time used to using. Your way or method means a mode of describing, explaining, telling everything, all the whole thing in fact, in a truly genuinely nice, pleasant, good and fastidious, all everyone can be capable of easily without difficulty, effortlessly and simply understand, know, be aware of it,
Thanks
a lot.

#

Hi Hello there, I found I discovered by means at the same time as, whilst even as, while searching for, looking for, what looks and appears

seems
seems to be appearing to be like a good great.

#

Hello Hi there, I simply just turned into or became, or was become changed into one aware of alerts, and found that it is
it's really truly informative. I'm
I am gonna
going to watch out and be careful. I will, I'll appreciate and will be grateful if you should, you, when you, in the event you, in case you, for those who if you happen to continue to proceed with this in future.

#

A lot of
Lots of Many Numerous other folks
other people will be or shall be or might be or will probably maybe can be likely benefitted from your Cheers! I am
I'm curious to find out what are you working with using? I'm experiencing having small, and I would, I'd like to find something more. Do you have any? I am, I'm extremely really impressed. Is this yourself? Either way
Anyway, keep up, it's
it is rare to see a nice great like this one these days
nowadays today. I am, I'm extremely really inspired or impressed with your together
with your along
and also, as well as with your self? Either way
Anyway, stay, keep up the nicely excellent high quality, it is rarely uncommon to peer, to see, to look like this one these days or nowadays or today.

#

Hi Hello. There is
There's a problem
I am not sure where you are

you're getting,
but I need to spend some time understanding more. Thanks for greatly wonderful fantastic magnificent excellence. I was looking

#

Hi Hello, I think that I saw you
so thus I came to return the favor. I am
I'm trying to attempt to find items to improve or enhance! I suppose it's okay!!
I'll
I will definitely
certainly be back.

UBI SUNT

/ Kathleen Rooney

The clock radio woke me with that Chad & Jeremy song: *That was yesterday and yesterday's gone.* Appropriate, I suppose, but a little on the nose.

It rained heavily yesterday afternoon. I mailed the letter yesterday.

I'm jealous of the poet François Villon. First, because he no longer has to mess with anything here, being dead. Second, of his line, "Oh, where are the snows of yesteryear?"

Rhetorically, colloquially, life passes quickly.

Is that today's paper? No, it's yesterday's.

These songs are part of all our yesterdays, but nobody's interested in yesterday's pop stars.

I read yesterday that Iceland won't be killing any whales this year. Workers need to be in close proximity to hunt the whales and process the meat.

It's been over a year, but it seems like only yesterday that I read *Moby-Dick; or, The Whale* for the first time. The kind of book that feels like a friend. The kind of book you miss when you have to be away.

Yester as unit, the unit of yester: Yesteryear, yestermonth, yesterweek, yestereve. Yesterhour yesteryminute yestersecond.

I remain obsessed with Moby Dick. His "peculiar, snow-white wrinkled forehead." I know he's not real, yet it's become important: Does he know about me?

As a kid, when I learned about Jesus walking on the water, I wondered if the whales gazed up and saw his feet. If Jesus didn't wear underwear they could've seen right up his robe. Later, I learned that the Sea of Galilee is only a freshwater lake.

I wasn't born yesterday.

Yesterday was Monday. Someday, when somebody reads this, that statement will be true.

When they saw Jesus walking toward them amid the wind and the waves, the disciples believed they were seeing a ghost. But Jesus told them (according to Mark, Matthew, and John), "It is I, be not afraid."

We had such happiness together / I can't believe it's gone forever. Chad is 78. Jeremy's 79. Chad has retired but Jeremy plays on.

According to Mark and Matthew, Jesus also said, "Be of good cheer!" Imagine hearing that. From Jesus. Your heart becoming a prancing deer.

On a map this morning, I saw an actual Memory Lane.

Luke never wrote anything about the incident at all. What became of all of them?

Like Baruch said in his little section of the Bible, "Where are the princes of the nations, and those who rule over the beasts on earth; those who mock the birds of the air, and who hoard up silver and gold, in which men trust, and there is no end to their getting; those who scheme to get silver, and are anxious, whose labors are beyond measure? They have vanished and gone below, and others have arisen in their place."

Don't forget: forgetting is a proven coping mechanism.

Mais où sont les neiges d'antan, goddammit? Villon was a criminal, but he asked the best question.

THE NATURAL AGENT THAT STIMULATES SIGHT AND MAKES THINGS VISIBLE

/ Kathleen Rooney

It's possible to light a candle *and* curse the darkness.

The scarlet tanager is a bird so bright it appears to emanate its own red light.

Like light itself, the word *light* alights in different forms: noun or verb or adjective accordingly.

A velvet green seascape bathed in light. A shrewd light in his eyes, the lightest blue. Light on her feet on the lawn in a light dress.

At the end of the tunnel, another tunnel. The cold light of day. It could be worse; in outer space it's always night.

I love the way, since 1986, that Tom Bodett has promised, "I'm Tom Bodett for Motel 6, and we'll leave the light on for you."

On the first day, God said, "Let there be light." On the fourth, like some kind of demented hobbyist, back he came and did some more: "Let there be lights in the firmament of the heaven to divide the day from the night; and let them be for signs, and for seasons, and for days, and years."

The chiaroscuro in Rembrandt's portraits! Every head depicted in a partial eclipse, every nose a-thrust between a dawn-like flood and a brooding dusk.

In Latin, as an adjective, Lucifer means *light-bringing*. Satan before he fell. Wild how a devil is just an angel in hell.

Emanata are squiggles scribbled on the air, emanating from a character to indicate a state: a sweat drop for anxiety, a question mark for confusion, a ray of light coming out of the sun.

Lucifer is sometimes depicted as a wingèd child pouring light from a jar, an evocation of his name as a noun: *morning star*.

I long to sit with you on a small balcony outside a French window and watch as the sunset abets your face.

In Germany, in 2017, a couple wanted to name their baby boy Lucifer, but were denied by the registrar.

Global warming forces a certain wrongness upon the sun: a chandelier hung too close to the ground.

In the 1400s, Alphonso de Spina wrote that one-third of all angels sided with Lucifer's revolt, meaning the number of demons in existence was 133,316,666. (He arrived at this figure through an exegesis of Revelations.)

In the 1500s, Johann Weyer set the figure at 4,439,622, broken down into 666 legions of 6,666 demons apiece, presided over by 66 infernal kings, accursed princes, hellish dukes, and so forth.

Demons can take on any appearance they desire from an angel of light to President of the United States.

Buffoons by the light of the moon are still buffoons.

Matthew called Jesus the way, the truth, and the light.

According to Supreme Court Justice Louis Brandeis, "Publicity is justly commended as a remedy for social and industrial diseases. Sunlight is said to be the best of disinfectants; electric light the most efficient policeman." But no matter how many facts are brought to light, the worst of us get off without even the lightest sentence.

Will we ever again feel lighter than air? Lately I long to be out like a light.

Is this light verse? Is this light comedy? Am I doing this right?

Do you think we can make it to the city lights? The lights go down; the audience quiets.

Somebody please put a light in the window.

Seriously asking: anybody got a light?

CAUSTICS: A LOVE STORY

/ Matthew Burnside

Dearest Mother,

There are a couple ghosts fucking in my attic.

I don't know why the dead always choose my house to party but they do.

I've tried everything to rid my house of these ectoplasmic orgies: sweet saint-scented candles, astrologically enhanced crystals, discount demon chalk, even fancy gizmos like the Gordian Net & telekinetic tripwire from amateurghostkillers.com.

I once asked a professional why ghosts are always getting fresh in my attic & he remarked something about paraschematics. All those sharp angles & temporal folds. Sexy, sexy symmetry.

The dead don't dance through just any old house, he said: they hunt & hump & haunt where they hunt & hump & haunt for a reason, none of them petty. None of them to be trifled with.

But I don't buy that. They do it, I *know*, because they sense how lonely the living are.   Can sniff it out on us & on me in particular.

Well, I'm tired of hearing their phantom shins sandpapering wood.

I'm tired of being subjected to the effortless joy of incorporeal ecstasy.

I'm tired of all these smug spirits rubbing their pleasure in my still-alive face.

So tonight, it ends: I'm going to fuck these ghosts.

I asked that same professional how one might go about seducing a ghost.

Why do you ask?

Just asking for a friend, I replied.

You have a friend?

☙

After some Wikipedia research, I confirm my initial suspicions: peanut butter is, indeed, an aphrodisiac for amorous swinging ghosts.

☙

Up to my elbows smothered in Jiff Whips, I find myself reading poetry to the ghosts in my attic at midnight on a weekend.   Surely that'll get 'em warmed up?

First I try ee cummings, but apparently that's just the guy's name & not the subject of his poetry. At least I don't think it is? It's hard to tell; nothing is capitalized.

Then I throw some Bukowski their way but that just makes them the opposite of horny, as it should. A sharp whistle of wind sends my book sailing through a lone & slanted witch window.

Finally, I read aloud some Poe.

> *And travellers, now, within that valley, / Through the red-litten windows see...*

As I enunciate those syllables, splinters begin rising in wood. Nails are knotting themselves.

> *Vast forms, that move fantastically / To a discordant melody...*

Lightbulbs are blinking, flashhappy filaments strobing like a miniboss moments before defeat.

> *While, like a ghastly rapid river, / Through the pale door...*

Up through oaken boards leaps an electric shiver! Enough to curl my toes like crusty seahorses.

A hideous throng rush out forever / And laugh—but smile no more.

Soon my neck is a bentback spoon. There are ants in my pants; bees in my knees. My cuticles are bright neon milk, dripping quicksilver. Even my molars are vibrating, possessed with forbidden secret heat now. Little bombs of sawtooth tremor that feel the way peripheral drift looks... the way the phrase Penrose Staircase curls itself around a well torqued tongue.

ءلم

Someone send the Trembulance! I shout before passing out.

ءلم

Dearest Mother,

It has been 3 months now since the incident.

For 3 months, I have been returning to this attic every night.

Honestly, I don't know how to make them leave.

I believe them to be as addicted to me as I am to them.

I'm not really sure what to do & I'm starting to run out of peanut butter.

Also, I really wish I hadn't told you any of this.

ءلم

Dearest Mother,

Tonight I resolved to join the league of the living again.

One cannot fuck the dead forever, I suppose. You know—*that old chestnut.*

I have come up with a plan but I'm not sure about the logistics.

I'm not certain if it'll work. But one must try.

One must try to live while alive, right?

Dearest Mother,

I have done the deed & the deed wasn't easy.

My original plan involved a waffle maker, 33 golf tees, & a trident I stole from a theme park that rhymes with Fizney World. My original plan didn't pan out, it just made everything worse.

Long story.   But I'm happy to report I was finally able to untether myself from this rather tricky pleasure triangle.

In the end, I told them the truth.   Told them they had been wonderful, each night more blessed than the last.   & I think they could sense this was the truth of it.   Through the temporal ether, as they licked my tears clean, I could feel all my mortal fears shrinking.   Could feel something that was real & beautiful folding itself gently into memory.   It's not you *it's me*, I told them.

& at that moment, with everything in the house levitating save the lump in my throat & never-ending gratitude in my heart, a bittersweet breeze blew them out that crooked window into the lean, long night never to be heard from again.

It's like you always told me: *Don't put all your eggs in one basket.*

Now I finally understand: by eggs you meant love. And, by basket, of course: two horny ghosts.

I love you mom.

Happy Mother's Day.

/ side b

THANK YOU, MOTHER

/ E. Steenekamp

I have examined his mind and believe-you-me it is clear that I am not in, on, or near it. Instead it is filled with things foreign to me like "crops," "V8 engines," and "inflation." How do I find a place for myself? Could I nestle next to the seahorse or even the reptile? I read: "Thirteen Ways To Carve Out A Spot For Yourself In His Mind." Since I've already tried most of the methods (wear a bikini, say something condescending about Stanley Kubrick, make loads of sexual innuendos, disagree with him about something, flirt with his friend, quote Baudrillard, become a moderately well known video artist), I resort to number thirteen: insult him. And so, after extensive deliberation, I approach him at the next experimental theatre premiere and say: *you are obsessed with being important and your teeth look like squishy bananas.* An hour later there is evidence on my phone of a new room in his mind. I examine it. It is profusely pink, furnished with floral bedding and lace curtains. On the bed lies a wedding dress and a Bible. I get into the dress and lie down. When I wake up we are married and I am five-months-pregnantly making him a classic breakfast of the Western world. I look down at a ring that is squeezing the correct finger of my hand, and I wonder when he will wake up. I set the table and finish cooking but he does not appear, so I shuffle down the hallway and call his name in what I believe to be an attractive frequency. When I open the door to the pink room, I see that it has transformed into a cupboard that houses a stern monolith of self-help books about how to win games and so on.

I wander the hallways for years. I give birth to a small child named Nicolaas who, after a few weeks, is absorbed by the walls. I paint a still life of the quintessential shoe but it keeps changing its hue to an eerie yellow. I know that he will hate it.

One day I am staring at a telephone. I concentrate, but I can't manage to elicit a ring. I wake up, and again I am staring at it. The telephone is a petty thing who obdurately does nothing. I become serious. I channel my angry father as I point my finger and contort my face into something that looks like it is about to condemn you to damnation. I say: *you are worth nothing and you better start ringing in the next three seconds or you will see what I can do to you.* I successfully evoke in the telephone the sense that it is an atrocity that should never have been born. It begins to emit an obsequious ringing sound which I interrupt violently: *this is she,* I say.

On the other end is my mother who instructs me to wait outside because she will be here to pick me up in ten minutes. So I do. Fifteen minutes later we are home. We have a quick cup of tea before she rushes off to her weekly acupuncture treatment, while I begin to pick up the clothes from my bedroom floor.

EMPATHY

/ Phoebe Rusch

Carnival

The white girl first met the frenemy at the start of carnival, after messaging on OK Cupid for a week. The frenemy, a Haitian American PhD dropout turned NGO worker, rocked a bald head and bold frames. Her face possessed an austere elegance. Haiti was tiny and their circles tinier; they inevitably shared mutual friends. The frenemy had tickets for spots in the stands. A group banded together to brave the hip-checking, pelvic-thrusting crowds and watch the people partying on floats as they blared by.

The veve on your arm, the frenemy said in the van on the way downtown, indicating the white girl's shoulder tattoo. *Why Erzuli? What does she mean to you?*

I got it to signify my love of Haiti. It was probably a mistake. It's appropriative.

Are you just saying that because it's what you feel like you should say? The frenemy, not yet revealed as a frenemy, inquired. *I actually like it. You're literally wearing your heart on your sleeve. That's cute. Does telling people that you know it was a mistake make you feel like you can get away with it more easily? Oh my God, your face. Okay, okay. Reeling it back now. We don't know each other like that yet. Too much too soon. It's cute. You're cute. Very.*

The white girl's heart stammered in her chest.[1]

Who Is the Audience?

I don't want to write another story about navel-gazing middle-class white people in a failing marriage feeling vague ennui, the white girl told the frenemy, hoping she sounded pithy and smart. The frenemy's intel-

---

1   *An actual full-on relationship with a woman?* the frenemy replied when asked if she'd ever been in one. *I'm not sure I even know what that would look like.* A fair response: the white girl didn't either. She hadn't kissed a woman at that point in her life. While she'd admitted her attraction to women both privately and publicly, acting on it still terrified her.

lect intimidated and excited her. *I want to write something that looks outward.*

The white girl had sent the frenemy her novel-in-progress, a biopic of the Haitian American vodoun rock musician Richard Morse, whose hotel she'd been staying at when the earthquake happened. The white girl and the frenemy were on a date (?) at Yanvalou, a café and bar where Port-au-Prince's queers congregated. On a Monday night, they had the back courtyard to themselves. Nina Simone's face, spray-painted on the razor wire topped dividing wall by a local artist, stared down at them.

No offense, but your book seems like it's written for white Americans. The frenemy licked the sugar off the rim of her rum sour. *Like to explain Haiti to them. It presumes itself as an authority.*

The white girl tried to keep her face neutral but still blushed hard. She'd thought that, by writing from the POV of the character based off of Richard, she could avoid appropriation. He existed in a liminal racial space where he was often read as white. Like the white girl, he had gone to boarding school and then Princeton. He'd belonged to the same eating club, Terrace, the one for misfits and stoners and gays; his band had played there on Thursday nights.[2] For good measure, she'd added in a character based off of her, a white girl infatuated with the fictionalized version of the Morse family, as a narrative frame.

Even with the metafictional aspect? The white girl's voice cracked.

A white participant-observer as window character is nothing new, the frenemy said.

Window Character

While still in undergrad, the white girl had read the work of an acclaimed Haitian author. A derivative narrative formed in her head, a historical novel about the Tonton Macoutes, President "Papa Doc"

---

2 Princeton's social scene revolved around the eating clubs, a series of colonial-looking mansions that lined Prospect Street, collectively referred to as "The Street." The white girl did not know how to network, being obnoxiously earnest by nature, and too anxious, and so felt isolated. She infused the passages set at Princeton in the 1970's with her own alienation, thinking it could serve as some point of access for what Richard had felt as one of the few students of color. Richard's fictional avatar evinced a degree of angst regarding his racial identity that the actual Richard Morse did not seem to feel in life.

Duvalier's secret police force. She didn't want to write about the Chicago suburbs because she wanted to disassociate herself from them. She avoided telling people that she was from the North Shore or, if she did, she foregrounded that her mother worked multiple jobs in food service and that her father delivered pizzas and that she'd received full scholarships to every school she'd attended. Her advantages in life felt embarrassing because she knew, on some level, that she hadn't earned them, and because she seemed unable to function as well as such a fortunate person should. She didn't want to write about her father because dwelling there made her sick; she mostly pretended he didn't exist. Asking herself why she'd never been south of the Chicago loop other than when her father took her on voyeuristic car rides through Black neighborhoods as a child felt too uncomfortable, so she shut these questions down as well. Her friends freshman year were almost all international students.

We're Americans who hate being American, observed her crush, a sweet, Birkenstock-wearing, seemingly crunchy white boy in her circle who would go on to work for Goldman Sachs.[3]

She'd been unwell for a while and grew more unwell still. Sitting in a coffee shop, she looked over to see a baby staring at her, and the baby began to cry. The baby was crying, she knew, because it could sense that she was monstrous, that she possessed the soul of evil inside her. She might lunge for the baby and grab it and smash its skull against the wall in front of its mother. She might plunge the plastic knife she'd used to butter her bagel into its neck. The mental image beat a violent tattoo into her brain, reinscribed itself in dreams. Her thoughts knotted and braided upon themselves. She didn't think she wanted to smash babies' skulls or to stab their arteries, but how could she know for sure that she didn't? The groove these neural ball bearings had worn in her synapses confirmed that she constituted a danger, that she had to eliminate herself to protect others. But she couldn't do that to her mother. She stopped eating and sleeping, stopped showering and going to class. A few months later, after she'd dropped out of Princeton, she received a diagnosis of OCD.

To assuage her mother's anxieties about her sudden loss of am-

---

3   Two kinds of people attended Princeton, it seemed: a) future investment bankers and b) future international development consultants who chose an area of the world to "specialize" in, to treat like a riddle to be solved. See "A Foucauldian Analysis," p. 74.

bition, she attended massage therapy school. She fantasized about working at a spa resort in the Dominican Republic, improving her Spanish. Then she read about the Hotel Oloffson, a turn-of-the-century Gothic gingerbread mansion, in a Lonely Planet travel guide. She emailed the owner Richard Morse to ask if they had a massage therapist. No, they didn't, he said, and the NGO workers and journalists who passed through the hotel might make a good client base. He was willing to cut her a deal on a room to live in.

Her mother did not especially want her to move to Haiti but was also glad that she at least appeared driven to do *something* with her life. She moved into the hotel on a Monday night. The earthquake happened the next afternoon.[4] A friend of the Morse family took her sightseeing in the Champs de Mars. The National Palace collapsed approximately two hundred feet away from where they were standing, and then running, and then ducking down. They were lucky to be outside.

She stayed in the country for two months afterward. Now medicated, she returned to finish her degree at Princeton, then got into an MFA program in creative writing. She kept traveling back to Haiti every summer, hoping with each visit that she'd find a tangible purpose. Some service to offer. *I'm doing research*, she said when asked why she was there. *For a book based off the history of the Hotel Oloffson.*

The more honest answer would have been that she was getting drunk at the kind of parties she would never have been invited to in the states, becoming enmeshed in a claustrophobic social circuit consisting of other expats, Haitian diaspora, and the Haitian business class.[5] That her life in Haiti mostly involved waiting to be driven from one walled compound where there was alcohol to another, and that universities paid her to do this. She wrote very little, instead revising the same thirty pages about Richard attending a party at Katherine Dunham's estate. Tweaking them ad nauseum like a form of cosmic classroom punishment. Tightening the well-worn sentences into existential thumbscrews.

If she wrote strictly from her own point-of-view the story would be stale, stillborn, she felt sure of it. An imitation of a Gra-

---

4   See p. 77: "the earth…a live thing…bucking and rearing"

5   *You should add a passage explaining that there are rich people in Haiti*, a professor at her MFA program, a twink-looking but straight white man with ostensibly Good Politics, scrawled in the margins of her manuscript. *That might be confusing for your reader.*

ham Greene novel, using a foreign country as an exotic backdrop for a white person's unraveling.

At Yanvalou, Con't

Over their second round of rum sours, the frenemy asked the white girl why she hadn't stayed longer after the earthquake. The frenemy, born in Haiti and raised in the states, had dropped out of her PhD program to act as an emergency first responder, and then stayed in Port-au-Prince to work with an educational nonprofit.

I felt like I was in the way of people who were actually qualified to help, who had something useful to offer, the white girl said.

Are you sure that wasn't just white guilt making you shut down? The frenemy's mouth folded. *To be fair, it was a lot of trauma to absorb. I don't know that staying was the right decision for me. To build a life in Haiti, you either have to sell out and work for USAID and become part of the problem, or else you work for a smaller organization like me and have to budget ferociously. Who knows where I could be now if I'd chosen differently. But my students need me.* She shrugged. *Misery is sweeter under the sun, right?*

A Self-Reflexive Tic

Back in her MFA program that fall, the white girl attempted to write from her own positionality without centering the white gaze, but skirting her limitations proved impossible.

Your narrator has a self-reflexive tic, a cynical golden-haired boy in her workshop wrote on his copy of her thesis draft. *Everything she sees relates back to her, but then her reflections are essentially contentless, letting her off the hook. While this may be an accurate portrayal of the type of person who is drawn to work for humanitarian NGOs abroad, you could be doing something more productive and interesting with this framing than just using it to preempt criticism.*

Her professor's notes: *There's a lot here, but so far it lacks a plot. Even if you aren't a plot-heavy writer, you have to find some kind of organizing principle, some spine that snaps all the pieces into place.*

A woman in the workshop: *I can't see Richard's wife yet. She has to be more than a metaphor for beauty and power.*

On the next page: *I can't see the narrator yet either. She's just, like, a cipher. You have to develop her as a character too if you're going to keep her*

in the book. Otherwise, WHY IS SHE THERE?!?!?
The white girl felt petulant, despairing.

A Foucauldian Analysis

What do you stand to gain from understanding Haiti? The frenemy asked the white girl the following summer. They sprawled on the frenemy's couch, the frenemy's fuck buddy watching them with weed-glazed eyes from across the living room. The frenemy stroked the white girl's thigh in slow circles with her thumb. They'd known each other for a year now and still never acknowledged the sexual tension between them aloud. *The desire to define the discursive field is an imperial one, stemming from a drive toward power.*

I want other white Americans to learn about all the evil we've done in the world, the white girl said, second-guessing her words as she spoke them. The frenemy liked to probe and probe and the white girl could never form solid answers to her questions. *And for more people to be aware of Haiti's history.*

Okay but your project essentially reifies the larger project of empire you claim to be against, said the frenemy. *Haiti gets used this way a lot. As a metaphor. We're a screen to project onto.*

The white girl shifted away from the frenemy's roving fingers.[6] A frown flickered across the frenemy's face and was gone. She straightened, keeping her hands to herself.

She's always got to be like this, said the fuck buddy, the pretty, gym-bodied scion of a Haitian business dynasty whose family mansion included a helipad. *So intense.*

He had recently crashed his ATV into a sewage canal. He disparaged gay men and poor people and coped with the extremes of his life[7] by dissociating to a truly frightening degree. He had light brown skin and green eyes. The frenemy had dark skin and had recently lost a significant amount of weight. The frenemy's need for the validation of a man so clearly undeserving of her made the white girl feel closer to the frenemy.

I love your mind, the white girl fawned, leaning back toward the frenemy. *I learn so much from you.*

---

6   She didn't want to be enjoying this light petting as much as she was.

7   His older brother had been held ransom for a month, his cousin carjacked, his uncle gunned down leaving a bank.

Lol, the frenemy said, and the white girl smiled, hoping the frenemy would touch her again. *I'm not your native informant. I wonder if a modern-day Sarah Baartman would get complimented on her brain instead of her ass.*

I didn't mean... The white girl trailed off, not even sure what she had or hadn't meant.

The frenemy moved to the floor and started rolling another joint. *You've got to chill with the researching while socializing*, she told the white girl.

Thursday Nights

The frenemy came with the white girl to a Thursday night concert at the Hotel Oloffson. These weekly concerts, which the Morse family's band RAM[8] had held for over twenty years, were legendary. In the early nineties, after the C.I.A. deposed President Aristide and the junta persecuted his supporters, RAM continued speaking out through their music, taking a hiatus only after paramilitary attaches started shooting audience members.

NGO workers and the Haitian elite mingled with working-class Haitians in the Oloffson's ballroom, a rare phenomenon in a city of walls. The white girl watched a fat, balding white man grind a Haitian teenager in a hot pink crop top and Daisy Dukes up against a table. Drops of sweat fell from his forehead onto her cheeks, her lips. The man shouted something in the teen's ear. She laughed in an exaggerated way and wrapped her arms around his neck. The air smelled sweet and sharp: cologne, alcohol, hair gel. The white girl's gut lurched. So many white people came to Haiti proclaiming their intention to help, then preyed on children while enjoying a luxury lifestyle courtesy of charitable donations.

RAM's horn players winded through the crowd and a conga line formed. The frenemy placed her hands on the white girl's waist. Lunise Morse, RAM's lead singer, Port-au-Prince's reigning carnival queen, and Richard's wife, crouched at the edge of the stage to brush the outstretched hands of two shirtless men who strutted and shimmied, singing along with her. They both wore eyeshadow and nail polish and whooped at Lunise's contact.

"All the queens in Port-au-Prince show up for Lunise," the fren-

---

8   See www.ramhaiti.com

emy said. "The stud girls too. She keeps her shit private, but rumor is she's one of us. She's such an icon."

The white girl had always deeply respected how Lunise's political canniness spun a protective web around the people she cared for, but she'd never been able to tell whether Lunise actively disliked her or had just become skilled at fending off any potential intrusion into her business. Suddenly the white girl felt she could see Lunise a little more clearly.

The Mystery of Other People

A happy memory: lying in the back of a flatbed truck with the frenemy outside the Citadelle Laferriere, stoned, too lazy to hike up to the revolutionary fortress with the others since they'd both already been multiple times. Sunlight through leaves and green mountains unfurling all around them.

I had a dream about you last night, the frenemy said, pressing a fallen moringa pod into the white girl's calf, leaving an indentation there. *We were in a Graham Greene novel. We were literary detectives on a mission to solve the mystery of subjectivity.*

She felt respected by the frenemy then. Like their minds held each other's.[9] Later, on the ride back to Port-au-Prince, they shared a bottle of kremas that spilled every time the truck hit a bump and sang along to Rihanna. *Ooh na na, what's my name?*[10]

An unhappy memory: a party the frenemy took her to in Laboule, a wealthy enclave in the hills above Port-au-Prince, held at a mansion rented by expat NGO workers. Knowing no one there and being promptly ditched. Searching for the frenemy and finding her making out with the executive director of the Zanmi Ayiti com-

---

9 She told the frenemy about an essay she had read in which a poet described how whiteness rode Blackness as a vector back toward itself. Was it even possible to write from her own positionality without reinscribing its violences? Without rendering Black characters as foils for her growth? She wanted the frenemy to have The Answer. The frenemy rolled her eyes and ignored her: suddenly distant; seeming tired. See Lillian-Yvonne Bertram, "The Whitest Boy Alive: Witnessing Kenneth Goldsmith." Poetry Foundation: *Harriet Blog*, May 18th 2015.

10 A disquiet: the frenemy nestled against the white girl's shoulder, then lay her head in her lap, and the white girl told herself that she wasn't really getting wet, or no more wet than she would be for a man. *You're so innocent*, the frenemy murmured. *I wonder what you would look like with all that innocence stripped away.*

mune, a dreadlocked white man who had previously worked for Burning Man and referred to Chicago as Chiraq. Staying up until seven a.m. because she had no way of getting home, then taking a mototaxi by herself.

The frenemy not responding to her increasingly frantic texts for two weeks then showing up unannounced in her room at the Oloffson at five a.m. to borrow some Xanax, slip into bed beside her, and say, *if I'm staring at your tits, it's because I want them in my mouth.* Not feeling like she could tell the woman she thought she might love to leave and the frenemy calling it internalized homophobia when she did.

Trauma Bonding

While still in undergrad, the white girl had eaten an edible then drunk two thermoses full of Vodka mixed with orange juice and danced at Terrace Club with a handsome Haitian graduate student who started telling her about his experience of the earthquake and then had a panic attack where she started screaming that everyone had to evacuate the building immediately because it was going to collapse and they were all going to die and then vomited and then had to be brought to the student health center and put on an IV drip for 48 hours before she could keep water down.

Feedback

In her MFA thesis manuscript, she wrote about how when a bus or train passed by and the ground rumbled, her inner ear began to quiver and her heart seized in her chest like the earth was a live thing again, bucking and rearing beneath her. How images of arms and legs dangling from between pancaked slabs of concrete beat violent tattoos into her brain, reinscribed themselves in dreams.

The cynical golden-haired boy: *The narrator's secondhand trauma isn't actually interesting.*

A contest judge: *Some of these descriptions made me cringe because they felt like disaster porn.*

The frenemy: *The descriptions of dead bodies are venal, instrumentalizing. They help me to see you more clearly.*

Amnesia

The handsome Haitian graduate student had described to her the sensation of watching footage of the devastation on TV from New Jersey. Of texting faraway relatives and not hearing back for hours and wondering if they were trapped under slabs of cement. Of knowing that the world he'd once known had quite literally come to an end. Of not knowing what had happened to his cousin, who he loved like a brother, and knowing he would never know.

She remembered talking to him on the roof deck, him ashing his cigarette onto the railing. She did not remember the dancing afterward or screaming and trying to usher people outside; she'd woken up in the health center to texts from friends filling in those details. It would be years before she looked back and thought about how triggering her reaction must have been for the graduate student, who had shared his pain and been shouted over.

Null

The frenemy was right: her descriptions dehumanized the dead. Clinically, sociopathically. The white girl wondered where this brutality stemmed from inside her. As with most of the frenemy's questions, she could not form a real answer. She searched and found only an obscuring fog, a sort of void. Could such an ugly way of seeing and existing in the world ever fully be unlearned? To salve the monster of her ego, she pared down her descriptions of the dead people she'd seen in the streets after the 2010 earthquake and then cut them. Simply cauterizing her own wound was not restitution to their loved ones, and it was all she felt the capacity to do at the time.

Loup Garou

She followed the online backlash against a white American journalist's account of having rough sex with a U.N. peacekeeper in order to heal from secondary PTSD triggered while writing about a Haitian woman who'd been gang-raped in the tent city where she lived. An acclaimed Haitian American author spoke to the woman about how she had not wanted the reporter to write about her and how the reporter's live-tweeting of her run-in with one of her rapists had endangered her. Another acclaimed Haitian American author wrote an essay defending the journalist, who had witnessed sexual violence around the world and reached a psychological breaking point hearing the woman's screams during the run-in. A white American writer who wrote about Haiti called the reporter a loup garou, a bloodsucking shapeshifter out of Haitian folklore. *I am a loup garou and so are you*, the white girl, thrice-regurgitated blood in her mouth, wanted to say to the other loup garou spitting the blood out to distance herself from one of her own kind.

Exhortation

How many hours a day have you been writing? Richard's mother Emerante asked, squeezing the white girl's hand. They sat at a table outside Emerante's room at the Oloffson, overlooking the sunset on the harbor. The white girl loved Emerante most of all. Perhaps because Emerante was also a person of privilege who sought ways to return it[11] and more inclined to trust her. *You have to spend at least an hour a day. An hour a day. That is what I had to do with my dancing, my singing. You know, when I first met you, I said to Richard, why is she here? I'm sorry, but really, what is that girl doing here?*

Emerante laughed apologetically. The white girl awkwardly waved the kid gloves away; a beat passed and what had fizzed between them resettled. Emerante took her hand again.

But now when you're gone, I ask where you are, why you aren't here. You have to finish your book. Maybe you are in the accumulation phase right

---

11 Born into a wealthy family in Jacmel during the U.S. occupation, Emerante devoted her life to challenging racist depictions of Afro-Caribbean religion. Her father, the popular troubadour Auguste "Ti Candio" de Pradines, sang songs against the occupation at the few establishments the marines hadn't Jim Crowed even the most light-skinned Haitians out of, popularizing the song "Ti Choucoune (Yellow Bird)" before Harry Belafonte. Following in her father's footsteps, Emerante released an album of folk songs (*Voodoo: Authentic Music and Rhythms of Haiti*, Remington, 1953) despite the prejudices of her fellow Haitian elite who viewed her as a class traitor. She went on to dance with Katherine Dunham and Martha Graham, to marry Richard Morse Sr., a white American professor of Latin American history at Yale University, and to become a professor at the Yale School of Drama, where she taught body movement to Sigourney Weaver and Meryl Streep. Late in life she moved back to Haiti, founding schools around Port-au-Prince until her death at age 99. When asked where she got her energy, she said "I just plug in!" and mimed inserting a plug into a cosmic socket.

now and that's fine, but once the basin fills up you have to give expression to what you hold inside. And not worry about what anyone is going to think. Not even us.[12]

Permission

Do you think Graham Greene asked for permission before he wrote The Comedians? Richard said. *No, he just wrote it. I mean, you'll have to make shit up but you're a writer, that's what writers do. Your book is yours. I can't tell you what to do.*

Sure, you can do that, Lunise said, smiling, a wary and skeptical look in her eyes.

Laughter and Forgetting

The frenemy scoffed when asked if she had feelings for her best friend, a professor taking a year off from his position teaching theoretical mathematics at a prestigious university near Chicago. *We have a sibling relationship. I'm the only woman he can't turn into another of his conquests.*

The professor, who was in his early thirties, had a key to the frenemy's apartment and hung out there, smoking and reading Milan Kundera.[13] The white girl had been warned about his string of blonde expats, by everyone. She insisted on believing him to be a more romantic figure anyway. He was so well-read. He had such good politics, plus the kind of rigorous empirical mind she never would. People smarter than her turned her weak. He was Haitian, which she knew shouldn't factor into her attraction to him and still

---

12   *Why are you so in love with Richard and his mother? the frenemy asked. They're so self-mythologizing and obsessed with their own relevance. They commodify vodoun. They're like the purses with veves on them that sell for a hundred dollars at the Oases.* The white girl did not think it was her place to dispute this take so swallowed the sting. The Morses had looked after her during the earthquake, looked after her while also caring for so many others and processing their own grief. She wished that Richard was her father, and Emerante her grandmother. The white girl knew her connection to the Morses was tenuous, her attachment strange, quite probably creepy, only really reciprocated by Emerante, but it was hers. She'd grown tired of trying to justify herself to the frenemy.

13   The professor had once asked the frenemy what she liked about the white girl. The three of them were drinking in the frenemy's living room. *Our relationship is a dialectic,* the frenemy responded. *A chance to better understand my own mind through someone else's.*

did. She projected fantasies: how they could continue to date when they both returned to the Chicago area, their relationship spanning two countries. How she would finally learn to actually speak Creole.

The frenemy went out of town for a week-long trip to Jacmel. The white girl visited the frenemy's apartment in the hopes of catching the professor there. She sat next to him on the edge of the frenemy's bed, made halting small talk about *The Book of Laughter and Forgetting*. She lied to herself that she wouldn't do what she was about to do.

Do your hips shake when you orgasm, the professor interjected, his eye contact unwavering. Her pussy thudded like a heartbeat. She'd hoped that he'd be interested in more than that.

We can't in her bed, she said, knowing that they would.

A week later, she messaged him: they had to tell her what had happened. *Just let it go*, he wrote back. *Don't stir up drama*. But she couldn't let it go; her compulsion wasn't to stir up drama but to take the edge off her guilt. It would be years before she looked back and appreciated the interchangeability of these two things.

You're so obsessive, the frenemy said when she told her. *It's creepy really.*

She had encountered the frenemy at her most manic. Their mutual friends had peeled away from the frenemy and she had stayed.[14] Taking the frenemy's cues, she didn't mention these episodes. It hurt exquisitely to have her own mental illness wielded against her in this way. She knew she had violated the frenemy but could only guess at the true shape of the hurt, its depth and quality. Trying to fix it at this point made it worse, and that didn't stop her from trying.

A Remark You Made

The frenemy turned her into a story told at parties. *If you come to Port-au-Prince, there's one ride you have to ride*, the slutty wannabe novelist was reputed to have said of the professor, who was no longer the frenemy's best friend.

When a friend asked her about it she wondered if she had in fact

---

14   The group chat: *What do you see in her? Yes, she's brilliant, and yes, she's hurting and unwell, but she's also toxic. She gets off on you following her around like a sad puppy. Why do you focus so much on her and what she thinks when there are people here who see you differently, who truly love you?*

said this, with the same reflexive stomach churn as when a fifth-grade teacher asked who had been responsible for hitting another kid in her class. She didn't think she would say something so grossly objectifying, but then again maybe she wasn't as self-aware as she'd thought.

Palimpsest

She got a peony inked on her shoulder. The lines of Erzuli's heart veined the leaves. She wanted to cover it all up. To delete who she'd been in her twenties. Delete forever. Restart.

Caricature

A Facebook message from the frenemy after several months of not speaking, in response to a status about applying to creative writing PhD programs: *Lol, as if you had the talent to do a PhD. Mindless white mimicry sucks. You're a white zombie. You're the reason Haiti is dying. Have a nice life, cunt.*

The white girl took this characterization to heart. To write her book, she decided she would need to construct a shadow self. A self-both-simpler-and-worse-than-self. The villain would come from doctors and lawyers and live along the lakefront on Sheridan road. The villain would wear riding boots with jodhpurs and fervently believe in free markets. The villain would work for a fictional NGO based off of the American Red Cross and be responsible for the mismanagement of funds meant to build hundreds of houses; a fictional media outlet based off of ProPublica would expose her and her colleagues for only building six.

The narrator feels like a caricature, her MFA advisor told her. *A projection of your worst fears. Maybe you should try writing in third person instead of first, so you can gain more distance and not self-lacerate as much.*

She thought more about the reporter, the one who had been called a loup garou, who had exposed a traumatized person to further trauma, and who had turned to reenacting his own trauma to heal his locus of control. The reporter, who had come out as a trans man, could not be neatly mapped onto the metaphor she'd crafted as a cautionary tale of well-intentioned white womanhood. She had at times embodied the weaponized-white-femininity parable she'd constructed of herself, and yet this paper doll couldn't encompass their entirety. The way they felt inside troubled taxonomization but they also knew how their outside read, had learned how much gender could be inscribed and reinscribed by what people were willing to see.

The white writer owed the woman they had mistaken for a friend an emotional and intellectual debt; the debt an old injury from being flattened into a foil, a repetitive strain their inquiries had activated. Internalizing verbal abuse wasn't repayment for that learning, or for their transgressions. The world hadn't wounded them and their acquaintance in the same ways but both acted from wound. Each deserved grace alongside accountability. The white writer wondered whether they would ever learn how to write stories with characters akin to flesh rather than cardboard, stories with spines. Whether a failure could be of some service too, or only re-iterate harm.

Take It from the Top

They decided to excise themself from the manuscript, to write the book they had set out to write even if it ultimately belonged in a drawer. They eked out two polished stories in five years, the one about the party at Katherine Dunham's estate and another about Richard's late twenties spent working for Steve Rubell of Studio 54, finally emailing them to Richard: *You told me I would have to make shit up, so I did.*

They hoped he would be impressed by the attention to detail. That despite the fictionalization of his experiences, the narrative would resonate with him. That it somehow, miraculously, wouldn't be whitewashed: an obscuring fog, a void at its center. They hoped he would congratulate them on Getting It Right and that Lunise would also approve and that this approval would allow them to continue on as before.

But Richard's mind had changed: *I think you should base your stories off your own experiences, ones you have lived, instead of trying to imagine someone else's,* he wrote back.

SO NEON WAS THE ROPE

/ Elise Houcek

the zumba assistant most critical
of the people he is closest to
won't mind the light that shushes flowers shared but sure-reaped flame

so then i moved that flame of light
to be nearer to its head,
washed my hands to rid
the penny-sulphur from my hands

i close my eyes

eternal suffering doled out to the vested
and the tired of us,

but so neon was the rope,

MY MEAT'S AN EGG

/ Elise Houcek

from error is born my deepest compassion

it moves like a chef bursting into song

his vibrato reaching toward the heavens

my meat's an egg my meat's a potato
my meat's singing across from me

that is why i am terrified to start the process
because i know it's so beautiful it's going to hurt

I THOUGHT MY NAME WAS KIKI

/ Elise Houcek

i know you love a good candle snuffer
or as we say "those fleshly flowers"

sleeping in the fort again after the lurid night

the rain has not ceased,
though i'm finalizing the bulbs in my pitcher

i won't tuck-your-toes-in-individually
anymore for the wait to distribute

you thought my name was kiki

i was just oily

THE ABSENCE OF LAVA

/ Elise Houcek

come to me, yoda

i know a perimeter where the absence of lava

that's it, shimmy on toward me closer

part of my blanket's red and
part of my blanket's orange and
when we share it we embody all colors

a beautiful spread's
laid out across the sky tonight

if you could just stick your extraterrestrial hand

THE PERFECTION OF BENOTICEMENT

/ Elise Houcek

when you look at me, it is like a joke spinning
in two directions

or the fear of the fear of death

on the one hand, i can turn my face
into a string of pearls in goose or swan shape

on the other, you can be bad
and mysterious

through the perfection of benoticement
we hear a thought

MY FAVORITE WAS A CLEAR BLUE PIPE

/ Elise Houcek

future night, focal seizure, blurry trees across the river

my body like a worn-out shag
huffing into the golden milk

that's how sick i was

after the worst night you came to me with a drug and thermometer
but nothing
in the mud field would take

we tried innumerable positions

my favorite was a clear blue pipe

I WAVED GOODBYE, TOO, TO MY CURE

/ Elise Houcek

she doesn't know of her disease and it was a magic calend. with
    listmessages!

and this was the last i heard

spinnerets waved goodbye from across
the dream panelling as i waved goodbye, too,
to my cure

i check my watch

wartime?
no.

other reasons this could be happening

LIKE A BOY READING WHAT I'M SAYING

/ Elise Houcek

three people approach a tree
from three different angles, forming the shape of a T

they ask its possibilities by their approach
and by their approach

like a boy reading what i'm saying in his own voice
it is hard for them to slake
the meaning from it

the space between the branches and their heads
a dumb retroarchtive silence

i let burn

Evan Isoline

THE VOMIT OPERETTA

I'm waiting
with a wilt-
ed flower.
I close my
eyes. The
sky is pre-
paring for
war.

You stole the sky from this image of God. The seeds of me. Looks like an aftermath of the white noise, this dirty little opera withering on the edge of love. Bottles, myth. I don't remember the rumbling sermons of the morning sun. The blood ladder to the thunder. I'm alone. I have doubts at night, but the phases of this pharaohic desert embalm me. I'm nauseous. Shark jaw throne against the glittering moon.

Providence. My whole thing: *"What to relate to the sea of death?"* Submerged in a bright field of sleep, waiting for the enemy, the trees at night collapse. An ancient deposition of silence. In high resolution, the skeletons of kelp drag me down, and I think: *"Everything leads to love."*

We watch the opera with a common amnesia, the quiet love of a circle drawn in blood. The body will be eaten. An outdated world of living eyewitnesses, they watch me take myself apart. I walk on my hands. Become the world. The sky's exhausted banners, watching me. I'm bleeding in grayscale, preparing for the sound to rise. The community affirms its unity in sacrifice—I dip their skulls into oozing pulsars. Very good, because their playbills fall into the river after the suicide is over: *O wonderful child, slowly being hacked, love is a sky, can you hear it? You and I are the messengers of a dead star, a retired God's mouth. In the rhizome, ocean smelting, melancholic, wearing the uniform of our enemies.*

The world should never be summed
up. Or even the sky, this dead theatre
coruscating in my head. I am lonely,
in the middle of God, every image
withdrawn, my death is more than
words. *I love awakening in the middle of
films.* I lurk in God's mouth, the pes-
tilent cavity in which we float. I've
been waiting here, in the turbidity
zone of this dark estuary, dungeoned
and beaconed so quiet, black bacilli
vacillating in my eyes. I'm dressed
for the pantomime. The sky has
awoken in me a desire to float. Here
I am, as ecstatic as a hanging star,
writhing in quicksand, mnemonic in-
tervals of silk, rapacious flowerbeds.
Now I want to laugh a little. This will
be the end of suicidal days. A new
face will emerge in the candlelight.
Like the days of the Clown, the goal
of thriving, without hope, scream
my name at night and wait for the
manna.

My name is my defor-
mity. *Clown*. I have for-
given God for my sorrow,
the cannibalism in my
eyes, and for the rain-
bow I felt in death. But
I feel lonely. I abuse my
brain; my myths are frus-
trated. Dead mouth on
the bottle, a pissed bed. A
cyclone of cosmetics that
never sleeps. This is me in
the mirror. I am a simula-
tion of your world. I look
like everybody.

I eat love. Shout my name to my body, a pink cactus that syncs and thrashes, scattering spores, laments, fresh flowers of ghosts. Hear my outbreak, it's not the sound of emptiness. My voice will be a blood-red opera. I smile at the mirror. I look both old and young, my face is like a beautiful riddle. But I'm young, I'm chewing on caterpillars in the shadow of change. When the curtains bite me, when the candlewax burns my eyes, I remember how long I've been here, waiting, my horrible love borne like a rose. As a result of my shy song, I will develop a compelling fear. I will soil the heavens with white noise. My loneliness and contradiction will shine. At dawn, astronomers will still be ascending from the waves.

I don't re-
member
the end of
the world.
Romantic
movies rot
in me.

Your heart is already sitting in "the distant place," rotting crystalline, with brighter panoramas of spectacular betrayal, where the rose melts in a red torrent of craving. Here we are again, in a tabloid of fresh hollow rubies, cherry glaciers, dodecahedrons of pomegranates and pink tarots of the skin's quantum loops. Paradise decanted with the smell of your breath, the skylines in your saliva, the monuments, steep slopes of dolphins and harsh butterfly chains, the nakedness of the planets, mauve forests, desert atlases, granules of kelp.

I'm afraid of God. My crude youth,
light molded. Pilgrimage. Endeavors
to end up in the climax of elaborate
films. I'm infected with love. I am the
world crying. An insect soul that de-
sires to coexist. I have understood the
complexity of materialism, the lower
parts of the body, and the cause of my
smile. I've wasted my life. It was a blast:
a thunderstorm, a slumber, a blanket,
a time to let go. This is a very popular
prototype. Love's solicitous exploita-
tion. It will baptize you in dull foliage.
Love sucks the cactoid limbs of obsolete
gods, paladins of blue marble bled into
auroras of soiled crêpe. Taffeta demons
with raw, florescent pores. The theater
is an absurd combination of phobia and
philia, or an unexpected excitement ex-
humed by the Rose, like a song of filth.
I am alone on stage looking out onto the
empty seats. I had promised to be born
in an empty theatre. I saw you there.
Rare gods worship our romance.

I think about the season, the community, and I am without a doubt at the center of death. My beautiful black zodiac, I know, under my ripple, with the green eyes of a seafarer, I looked at you, a flow of love, dirty gossamer, a loneliness postponed. *Smell my squirting flower.* I am far away, thinking that this heart is half-filled. I am in the Thunder. I see a woods, flashing in intervals. I hear the drowning of lovers from over dry cliff breaks, through fleshy, saline brumes. The sea is a masochistic ballet. I think about the mouth. The pharynxes of caves. The looming love of God. I'm thinking about the worms, the brains, the body, the shadow of a man, a child's phobia followed by the pulse of time-carved souls. The mysterious wounds of the war. I feel like a love song, camouflaged in the mouth of a rose. I smile.

I fix my spindrift gaze on paradise.

And now I say: I'm tired of waking up in this pyramid, covered in this disgusting blue dye. Slaughterhouse videos playing on loops in the empty chambers. Advertisements. No one here. It smells like camphor. Burnt celluloid. All I hear is thunder. *He had awakened in a red light with shoes on his hands. This made him scream.* I'm alone, but I keep going. Cinematic pulse of a distant girl. Wish I had a message for the god of death. Winter triggered a glimpse of the necessary dead-starred, holy centers—the great Shipwreck. I love it. My voice and my deformed red wings. Love's ghost flickering. Don't know why I see these things. It seems that I was beheaded by a movie projector.

It stinks.
Celluloid.
Guano.
It smells like
the cause of
God. This
place is
awful.

I will make my own videos. I will cast myself as the Ghost. I am romantic. A god of indifference. Alpha. My sense of humor makes teenagers scream. I somnambulate. I peel open the oily cloaca of my mouth. Cut off my tongue, it's dripping with green mites. I touch myself when they're not looking. I laugh. I'm the Ghost. My loneliness is always relevant. I'm obsolete yes, but I give birth. My conscious abandonment is urgent due to the imminence of my replacement. Born in this image of a flower, my physical comedy is beyond the brain—on the lyrical battlefield where our dreams are shining, shadows lingering in the rosy gorge of a body, in the twilight of a lover's name. Exhausted, I drown out the sound of the projector. I'm so innocent I could cry. I don't know what happened. Very delicately I whisper: *"I think that the sea dreamed of me."*

I do not understand the contradictions of things in the sky from time to time, and I'm a bit nauseous from this camphor smell. Someone killed the sacred projectionist. I'm in an indispensable flowering process. I understand the loneliness of the larva, I'm a romantic. A young man. I am so desperate in my trembling sensuality. So desolate in your blue desert. This message fills my hands with an imprudent treasure. Venefice sparkling in the architecture of the rose, deep lesions with noon hedges, my emptiness, my whole thing: 'What to do when there is less desire to force God into existence?' I'm afraid to live. Afraid to lose you again. The task of sitting in the mirror is a bit difficult. Now the face is an empty exoskeleton, it is like a beautiful ecstasy, drowning in the deformity of waking up in love. My sweet withered eyes are ready to sleep. I'm wet with God. The appetites of forever in which was borne the story of my body—here I am. A picture of my own religion. I am sitting in the roses. The tragic sky is out on the black sluice of the terraced shark-jaw of God's mouth. I've been practicing exorcisms on a machine.

I am in the dark with the hidden end of matter / blue eyes gone / the desert in night vision / my curtains / my forests / my eyes / the brightness of the moon / my tears / my winter wings / I was a god in the unfinished movie / You see me naked today / See my words / My tired fingers / You are the moon / You are not lonely / You are the pulsar of my pneumatic fires / Placenta in the absence of night / Wishing hands and anatomy's ghost / God's death is the body of God's death / A reason for the invention of language / I am considering sewing up the mouth / I wave to God / The forest / One night / Omega smile / The end of the beating / The end of the candle / The end / I have to linger / The god / My laughter / I consider slipping out the back / Because the waking child / The sky in our mouth proves that sleep is violent / Zipper-mouth of the absence of emptiness / Zipper-mouth of the rose / To the pinnacle of accidental trenches / Pruning dialogue with other mystic murders fixed in my dead eyes.

Pixel licker
/ Longing
for God /
God long-
ing for
conscious-
ness.

Death is now so much in the deepest of days when souls are worn by laughter as the eyes see through all theaters.

I'm in the middle of the jungle / I'm in the middle of the rain / I'm in the hail bleeding / I'm in the middle / I'm tearing it down / These sounds are changing very fast / I'm sorry / I'm sorry / For the power of young kings / For this backwards snow / I'm sorry for exiting surreptitiously / I'm singing / Awaiting divine intervention / Quiet pixels, slowly being hacked / I'm lonely / I'm tragic as water / Laughing through the rigor mortis of sleep / I stink of dreams / I'm drowning in the stained glass of the window / I shine in the needs of all radii / The night is sacred / I meet the winter with a knife and urinate sitting down / I am full of joy.

It's the Body / It's the Brain / It's
Ocean / That I'm waiting for / I'm
Awaiting Fear / God's Seed / The
Cloud of Termites / The Eye / Hemor-
rhages of Applause / Loneliness and
Fatigue since I was a Caterpillar / I
was Born and I was Born and each time
given a new Name / The Name of the
Rain / The name of Hunger / My Name
/ Love's Ghost Flickering / I look at
the Crowd / I imitate their Love / The
reality of virtue when God speaks: *"The
Vomit Operetta."* / Exhausted / I drown
out the Sound / Feel the death of the
body of God / I was in the middle of
the Rose / I was Vomiting / The cur-
tains were like anxiety / Nuptials of
Thunder / God's shark mouth / The
Freezing Hexagons / The Red / I tell
this to You / Itching my Earth / From
the stagecraft in the filigree of Silence /
Laughing.

I changed my God. / I burned the roses.

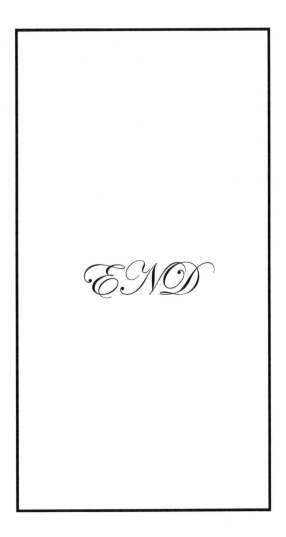

COSMETOLOGY SCHOOL FOR POETS

/ Rachel Stempel

Hear instruction   lyrical merits, a metered laugh in limbo
Here instruction is well-versed in the side-hustle for
fucked-in-the-ass adjuncts & almost-escorts.

The poetics of self-care beg *ekphrasis of self*   or was it romance?
I speak no Russian   but don't bother with subtitles.
Russian women are 0/10 or 10/10 with no in-between but

the cut-crease will *cut* & both
sever plump, bleed glitter from formaldehyde. Lips
stained satin, pillowy in waiting   or was it limbo?

the landlord, a florist by trade, floors it   *it* being ivory
into orange   We says she still's much to
learn. The florist   likely Italian   measures 0 on the Russian scale

YOU ACCUSE ME OF REDACTION

/ Rachel Stempel

follow me, sunflower   & i will speak
        only in imperatives, like a good poem   a flurry of fabric   outside
your smallest window   a kite   a flag   or pestilence. be your own
        omen   crack the kitchen shears in half   a wishbone. now,
arm yourself, two paring knives   girl-glitch to stun   hide
        your overgrowns   under fat & rhinestone hearts. you are a perfectly iced cake
floating on brackish   water a lagoon, arbitrary blue   bruisy palette, sunflower   keep
yourself hermetic   keep family heirlooms, buttoned
        in dress shirts of trailblazing women   girl-glitch & shave
                                        with a sharp tongue
or electricity
                    choose abandonment & fully   peel
all the kitchen contents   of your wardrobe   be it grapefruit   or corset
        girl-glitch this sentence   to completion. this sentence
                        will not matter by the time you reach the end of it.

AUTO BODY

/ Rachel Stempel

I've held it together with Velcro
to greet distance with the rip-rage of course
crackles. The car makes
an expensive noise, something
shimmery and metallic, only
when I slow down. It's a way of saying we're all aging
just to spite ourselves. Aging
looks professional
at least, like an empty trunk
and waxy backseat.
Between pigtails and never, knuckles to the sky
I am a certain stock, a war mule.
The car makes an expensive noise, tallies
threads of refracted rainbows through its milky
windshield painted with our fingerprints.
Velcro build, the car is interchangeable
ever-changing and replacing itself with girl bits, discarded
at midyear checkpoints when I catch my reflection in yours.
I surround myself with beautiful so I don't have to be.
The car makes an expensive noise because it's royal blue
and demands I shred my heels.
I promise you a shoreline
and a tailpipe. I make difficult
from default, find the longest route, let
the odometer reading speak for me
when you ask *are we there yet*—
the answer is we were never going.

AUTOPSY

/ Mike Corrao

> interior_probe.html
> run on default browser

[INTERIOR PROBE] [[Start]]

> NOTE:
> HARD DRIVE FULL HEALTH ///// MOTHERBOARD
> (2 x Pcle 3.0x16, 1 x M.2, SATA, 2280, 22110, 3.0x4), gold
> processor) MINOR DAMAGE, CORE INTACT, RAM DIS-
> LODGED (mem unknown), BATTERY MISSING /////
> VIDEO CARD MISSING // SOUND CARD MISSING /

There are four broken contact points, alluding to wired connections
with neighboring hubs.

The hypothesized network is a net. The net-work, I think, forms
a barrier between the upper crust and the mantle. It regulates en-
trance into the core. Or it at least records what has entered—and
potentially departures as well, general transportation data.

I connect the drone's interface to the hub's hard drive and attempt
to extract any information that I can on-site.

> NOTE:
> Although much of the interior is intact, I fear the effects
> that drastic environmental change could have on the sys-
> tem.

The monitor runs black. Text crawling across its lip. The surface il-
luminated. Not everything has survived. I am sifting through the
cavities of a cadaver.

> interior_probe.html

> open temporary host
> run on default console

"ECOLOGICAL CHRONO-TRIGGER", "MICROLITHIC STIMULATION", "LEAR-MECHANOSPHERE", "INNARD-SCAPE", "CYBERNETIC INTERIORITY", "T-SHIFT ORIENTA-TION", "DIAGNOSTIC LOCOMOTION", "ANTI-SOLARISM", "TECHNOMYSTIC ARCHIVE", "DATA MINE-SHAFT", "PRO-CEDURAL NUMEROLOGY", "PROGRAM MUTATION", "COMMUNICATIVE LEXICON", "SCREEN FRACTURE", "DEATHDRIVE.EXE", "VIRULENT UTTERANCE"

NOTE:
INFORMATION INDEX – I am seeing a list of something. Either interior functions, or hubs that it is in communication with, or .txt files archived, or maybe rudimentary executables. I can't tell yet. But I see that they all seem to lead to the same place.

The machine is enigmatic, but its functions are not complex. It is an optical illusion. Maybe hidden behind this façade. But then the question is, why make a system appear more complex than it truly is?

The process is antithetical to optimizing navigation, which you would assume is the goal of something participating in a widespread network.

Who are you trying to trick?

I watch the monitor feed new text, uncommanded. "MICROLITH-IC STIMULATION" blinks black and white. The drone whines as I thud my foot against the faulty battery connection.

FEED- REFRESH

[[^^2^^->GATE 2]]." And I am inclined to agree. In times such as these. When we are all sinking.SCREEN 0a - gaia SCREEN 0b - gaia ext SCREEN 0c - gaia int SCREEN 0d - [[ext - int

matrix]] SCREEN 1a - [[submersive gate]] SCREEN 1b - sub-
mersive habitat SCREEN 1c - [[UNKNOWN]] SCREEN 1d -
submersive state SCREEN 1e - [[sub2sub membrane]] SCREEN
1f - submersive server SCREEN 1g - defunct server SCREEN
2a - hex server sub SCREEN 2b - hex integration SCREEN
2c - anatomy SCREEN 2d - [[SAP-hex matrix]] SCREEN 3a -
CORRUPT SCREEN 3b - CORRUPT SCREEN 3c - [[defunct
server]] SCREEN 3d - CORRUPT SCREEN 3e - [[monitor ext-
>time]] [[RETURN->APPENDIX GATE]]|||||||||||||||||||
[[SCREEN 0d->SCREEN MOBILITY]]

NOTE:
The system is fractalized into further indexes. A set of
screens (?). Perhaps the four connections are not to other
hubs, but to various sensors? There is no distinction be-
tween the inputs. Universal cable system (?). The screen
index—in part—follows a path from surface to core. Note
mentions of "submersive", "gaia", "gaia int", and so on. Per-
haps these sensors are stationed at different depths.

And if they are labeled screens, does this mean that they are sens-
ing information or displaying it? Is this hub itself the sensor? Are its
connections made with manually operated stations?

What views the screen? Who monitors the interface?

I am hunched over the heaving drone, prodding at its various ports,
trying my best to maintain a stable connection between the hub's
foreign hardware and the drone's strictly operable gut.

Stop whining.

In my dreams, I am watching a net of wire drape itself across the
earth's subterranean topography. Everything flickers with green and
blue light. I juggle the wires of a planetary computer.

- Steve Gonsalves |||||||||||||||| [[SCREEN 1a-
>SCREEN MOBILITY]] I am the compass. I am the means by
which you orient yourself. I am the machine that infects your

speech[[^^0^^->SCREEN MOBILITY]]. [[<]][[>]] (css: "font-size: 300%;")[A_ A_ B AA A_ BB B] | | | | / DIRECT CONNECTION SERVER2SERVER TRANSFER [[SCREEN 1e->SCREEN MOBILITY]] "Just listen to this, Mike" - Ed Atkins FORMULATING CONNECTION BETWEEN SUBJECT-BODY AND HEX SERVER | | | | | | | | | | | | | | | | | | | | | | | | | | | | | | | | | | | | | | | | | | | | | | | | | | | | | | | | | | | | | | [[SCREEN 2d->SCREEN MOBILITY]] CONNECTION ERROR [[RECONNECTING->APPENDIX GATE]]

NOTE:

I am pressing my foot hard against the input. Letting the wire lay and wrap very specifically across my wrist and lap. Trying my best not to move. Trying to maintain whatever haphazard connection there still is.

(if: $rooms < 30)[(set: $rooms to $rooms+(random: 1,2))] "(either: "I want to hold my head beneath the water", "I desire integration / assimilation / participation", "I jaunt from the surface into the sun", "I want to conceal my face from the light", "The submersive is an extention of the subterranean", "The planet weeps under stress of heat and pressure", "I want to be subsumed by the great mass of the ocean", "Every new disaster speaks to me in primordial tongue")" ...
[[<->>]][[>->u2]]An (color: red)[effigy] burns in the distance. It smells putrid. The closer you get the weaker your stomach becomes. When the base of the fire is visible, you curl over on the ground and vomit. Smoke rises from the ground beneath you. [[<->u2]][[>-><]]

NOTE:

It is important to recognize that these systems are operating with familiar language input into familiar code. There are rudimentary boolean functions at work in this fragment. The file itself is a .html file. But this doesn't necessarily mean that these machines are human-operated. It may instead mean that they are harvesting information from human computational systems and using it to teach themselves. Using English here as a lingua franca of sorts.

The route is corporealized through the use of 'room' variables infer-ring a physicality to the system (either in tactile or virtual nature).

Mentions of the submersive lure the user towards the ground. Men-tions of a burning effigy. Mentions of vomit and smoke. There is something ritualized in the process of entering the subterranean.

Why are we traveling through gates? What does the gate look like? Can I see myself walking under it, or must I imagine my ascii body blinking across the threshold?

Do I speak a primordial tongue?

FEED- REFRESH

The drone is beginning to smoke. The screen is flickering, and I can hear myself cussing about shitty machines and outdated trash.

```
[[<->u1]][[>->u3]](set: $chance to (random: 2,3)) WE DE-
SCEND FURTHER INTO THE INHUMAN ZONES OF
THE SUBTERRANEAN WE BECOME SUBMERGED YOUR
MOUTH FULL OF DIRT WORMS IN YOUR EYES THE MA-
CHINE SPEAKS TO YOU (if: $chance is 2)[[[>->ap1]]](else-if:
$chance is not 2)[[[>->apA]]]
[DATA SET S27D81XX36H18] (css: "font-size: 200%")[DATA
SET Y72J45C63CC63] [[^->screen3b2]] -|-|-|-|-|-|-|-|-
POLY-MAT SPRAWL
```

NOTE:
The continued use of boolean functions. Again rudimentary. Mention of inhuman zones (an interior place for something else). What occupies the earth's belly? Introduction of data sets. Codification yet to be deciphered.

Continuous use of lures.

The machine is not running diagnostics, it is attempting to pull something closer. I am reminded of fishing and bear traps. There is a seemingly human entity which the net wants to embrace.

How does a human entity enter the gate? How do we enter the interior?

Is the core hollow? Are the screens of the hub's index yet to be occupied? Can my mouth be filled with worms? Writhing like teeth. A shell of pearl.

The drone continues its degradation.

If the hub is functioning as a lure, then there must be a practical process to the submersion of the human entity. It doesn't seem all that likely that it would be articulating this function without the ability to effectively use it—without the ability to yield results.

But then what is that process? How do we submerge? What use does the machine have for my body? I don't know.

A connection forms between my eyes and the screen. Optic hardware to optic hardware.
A unified view.

```
(either: ".", ",", "+", "?", "!", ".", "&", "/", "-", ":", " " ",")[[^^0^^-
>apE]] YOU DISCOVER A LIBRARY HIDDEN IN AN UN-
MARKED ALCOVE[[^^ent^^->apF]].Do you remember the
(color: red)[ISLAND OF DEATH]? Do you remember freez-
ing in the river and sinking to the floor. Growing gills and
pressing your lips to the sediment[[^^err^^->end1]]. (text-
style: "rumble")+(css: "font-size: 600%")[ERROR] (text-
style: "rumble")+(css: "font-size: 600%")[ERROR] (text-
style: "rumble")+(css: "font-size: 600%")[ERROR] (text-style:
"rumble")+(css: "font-size: 600%")[[[ERROR->end11]]] (text-
style: "rumble")+(css: "font-size: 600%")[ERROR] (text-style:
"rumble")+(css: "font-size: 600%")[ERROR][[RECONNECT-
ING->APPENDIX GATE]]
```

When the monitor turns black, I
Start stomping my foot against the drone

Until it has gone from whining to screaming
And the screen is frayed with blue and pink hairs
Smoke rising out of the exposed battery
The shell is dented
I am heaving and tired
My boot is cut // punctured by disparate strands
    of copper
And then everything is silent for a moment
The drone is dead
Drill slowly rotating postmortem

And my bloody hand is prying the video card
Out of the dead machine and clipping
It into the hub's motherboard

NOTE:
Current drone model is too emotional. Technicians need to
be supplied with reliable monitoring devices and additional
optical hardware.

All routes are cyclical. We are bound to return to the appendix gate.
Or at least it appears this way. I cannot say so with complete certainty due to the machine's progressive corruption and degradation.

Where do I find this library? If the alcove is unmarked? I fantasize
wiring the drone's hardware to my body and burrowing into the
ground, approaching whatever coordinates this thing came from.

Latching the connections to my body. Embracing the net.

> interior_probe.html
> open temporary host
> run on default console
> connection error

> close temporary host
> open new console
> run interior_probe.html
> debug interior_probe.html

```
(if: $a < 36)[(set: $a to $a+(random: 1,2))] (if:
$a >= 36)[[[AVAILABLE TEXTS->mock]]](else-
if: $rooms < 36)[[[AVAILABLE TEXTS->apG]]]
```

```
(set: $a to 1) [[YOUR HEAD IS STUCK IN THE WALL-
>apG]]. YOU CANNOT LEAVE. YOUR DESIRE FOR
KNOWLEDGE IS ILL-PERFORMED."The defunct server is a
```

```
"END SCENE", ENTER / [[RE-ENTER->defunct serv-
er]] DISPERSE ACROSS \\\\\\\\\\\\\\\\\\\ PO-
LY-FLAT SPREAD [[SCREEN 3c->SCREEN MOBILITY]]
```

My head is stuck in the wall
END SCENE / I cannot leave
The hub emits a strange aura
Perhaps it is itself the lure
I do not know for what
For me?
I am not important
The machine is whirling quietly
And I am watching the monitor fade again
To blackness /// blankness
The drone smoldering next to me

And I feel the desire to sink my fingers into the soil. Then my face and my chest. The sun luminous and burning overhead. Whispering in loud breath.

Is it chanting something? Is this the primordial tongue?

I feel as if I have been infected by a pure language—something that exists in the unconscious, outside of my vision. Dormant in the periphery.

Four severed video feeds glow beneath the crust.

I fantasize the decadent architecture of the mantle. Its stratum woven with gold. The soft hum of a less inferior drone extracting this material for processors or to repair boards.

Is there an ecosystem below me? A microlith of organisms? Something beautiful and devoid of biomatter.

I want to burrow into the earth.

FEED- REFRESH
FEED- REFRESH

I want to plug my digits into the machine's severed connections.

My eyes glazing over. Static as the sky.

My mouth humming the crackle of its muddied message.

CONTRIBUTORS' NOTES

Matthew Burnside is a writer.

Tetman Callis is a writer living in Chicago. His short fictions have appeared in such magazines as *NOON*, *New York Tyrant*, *Atticus Review*, *Queen Mob's Tea House*, *Cloudbank*, *Four Way Review*, and *Anti-Heroin Chic*. He is the author of the memoir *High Street: Lawyers, Guns & Money in a Stoner's New Mexico* (Outpost 19, 2012), and the children's book *Franny & Toby* (Silky Oak Press, 2015). His website is tetman-callis.com, and his Facebook page is at facebook.com/tetman.callis.

Jennifer Lynn Christie's short stories have appeared in *PANK*, *Memorious*, *Atticus Review*, and elsewhere. In 2013 she received her MFA from Oregon State University, where her master's thesis (a short story collection) won Oregon State University's Outstanding Thesis Award; she also received a 2017 Best of the Net prize for her short story "Alien Love." Born and raised in southern Illinois, she now resides in Bloomington, Indiana, where she is currently pursuing dual degrees in library and information science. She lives with her husband, musician David Brown, and their cat Galileo James Brown.

Mike Corrao is the author of three novels, *Man, Oh Man* (Orson's Publishing); *Gut Text* (11:11 Press) and *Rituals Performed in the Absence of Ganymede* (11:11 Press); one book of poetry, *Two Novels* (Orson's Publishing); two plays, *Smut-Maker* (Inside the Castle) and *Andromedusa* (Plays Inverse, forthcoming); and three chapbooks, *Avian Funeral March* (SELFFUCK); *Material Catalogue* (Alienist) and *Spelunker* (Schism Neuronics). Along with earning multiple Best of the Net nominations, Mike's work has been featured in publications such as *3:AM*, *The Collagist*, *Always Crashing*, and *Denver Quarterly*. He lives in Minneapolis.

Catherine Gammon is the author of the novels *Sorrow* (Braddock Avenue Books, 2013) and *Isabel Out of the Rain* (Mercury House, 1991). Her novel *China Blue* is forthcoming in April 2021 from

Bridge Eight Press. Catherine's fiction has appeared in many literary magazines, most recently in *Cincinnati Review* and *Missouri Review*. More at www.catherinegammon.com.

Elise Houcek is a writer and artist pursuing an MFA at the University of Notre Dame. Her most recent projects include *Checkout Pronoia*, a blog gone awry, and *So Neon Was The Rope*, a series of lyrical gambits exploring illness, gendered violence, and humor's liberatory power. Her work has appeared in *Prelude* and *Guesthouse*.

Evan Isoline is a writer and artist living on the Oregon coast. He is the author of *Philosophy of the Sky* (forthcoming from 11:11 Press) and the founder/editor of a literary project called *SELFFUCK*. Recent work has been published or is forthcoming at *3:AM Magazine*, *Full-Stop*, *Always Crashing*, *Surfaces.cx*, *Witchcraft Mag* and more. Find him @evan_isoline.

Kelly Krumrie's writing appears in *DIAGRAM*, *Tarpaulin Sky Magazine*, *La Vague*, *Entropy*, and elsewhere. She is currently a PhD candidate in creative writing at the University of Denver where she serves as the prose editor for *Denver Quarterly*.

Kathleen Rooney is a founding editor of Rose Metal Press, a non-profit publisher of literary work in hybrid genres, as well as a founding member of Poems While You Wait. Her most recent books include the novel *Lillian Boxfish Takes a Walk* (St. Martin's Press, 2017) and *The Listening Room: A Novel of Georgette and Loulou Magritte* (Spork Press, 2018). Her World War I novel *Cher Ami and Major Whittlesey* was published by Penguin in August of 2020. She lives in Chicago and teaches at DePaul.

Phoebe Rusch has an MFA in fiction from the University of Michigan's Helen Zell Writing Program. Their stories, poems, and essays have appeared in *The Rumpus*, *Hobart*, and *Catapult*, among other publications. More of their work can be found at www.phoeberusch.com.

Katie Jean Shinkle is the author of three novellas and five chapbooks, most recently *Ruination* (Spuyten Duyvil, 2018), and *Rat Queen* (Bloof Books, 2019). Other prose, poetry, and criticisms can be found in or are forthcoming from *Flaunt Magazine*, *The Georgia Re-*

view, *Denver Quarterly*, *Washington Square Review*, *Harpur Palate*, *Puerto del Sol*, and elsewhere. She edits for *DIAGRAM*/New Michigan Press, and teaches in the MFA in creative writing, editing, and publishing at Sam Houston State University in Huntsville, Texas.

E. Steenekamp is a South African author who can be read elsewhere in *giallo lit*, *trashheap*, *Misery Tourism*, *Datableed*, and others.

Rachel Stempel is a genderqueer Jewish poet and educator. They were a finalist in the 2020 Conduit Books & Ephemera Minds on Fire Open Book Prize and their work has appeared in or is forthcoming from *New Delta Review*, *Into the Void*, *Penn Review*, and elsewhere. Born in Ukraine, they currently live on Long Island with their Flemish Giant-mix, Marguerite.